ASCEND

A Coach's Roadmap for Taking Your Performance to New Heights

By Ed DeCosta

Your Future Self

ISBN: 1494388804
ISBN 13: 9781494388805
Library of Congress Control Number: 2013922501
CreateSpace Independent Publishing Platform, North Charleston, South Carolina

Contents

Acknowledgements

ASCEND is my first book. It began three years ago, on January 21, 2011 in West Palm Beach, Florida. I was meeting with the incomparable Dr. John C. Maxwell, the New York Times best-selling author and world-renowned leadership guru. We were discussing my potential involvement in a collaboration he was planning with Paul Martinelli and Scott Fay. John asked me "Ed, have you written a book?" When I told him that I had not, he playfully poked me in the chest and asked again "Do you have a book in there, a message that you need to send?" "Yes, I do," I replied. "Well," said the man that had, at the time, sold over 20 million books, "that message isn't doing anybody any good until you write it down and put it in a book." I am grateful for John's simple yet profound advice and for our subsequent partnership on the John Maxwell Team.

I am supremely grateful to Paul Martinelli and Scott Fay for creating the John Maxwell Team and for selecting me to be part of it. It continues to be one of the pleasures of my life to collaborate with them, as well as with my amazing teammates Melissa West, Roddy Galbraith and Christian Simpson.

Thank you to Justin Spizman and Joel and Lisa Canfield, who showed me the way, answering countless questions beginning with "How am I going to do this?" You led a blind man through the desert of the book writing process. A big thank you to Brian Allman, the greatest man I've ever known. He told me to say this, but it actually is true. *Ascend* would not have happened without the creative genius of Jim Matuga and Mike Arbogast of InnerAction Media. They come up with all of my greatest ideas, then they tell me.

I am filled with gratitude to my parents, Jim and Millie, and my brothers, Jim and Mike, who shared with me the crucible of South Boston that gave each of us the permanent chips on our shoulders and the absolute refusal to quit. I would not trade my upbringing for anything. "Look Mom, I'm an author!" (Boston accent removed.)

Finally, I want to thank my beautiful wife Linda and our wonderful children David, Brian and Laura. They have been and will continue to be the greatest sources of love and inspiration for me. I have been blessed beyond measure to be Linda's husband and their father.

There are so many other people that I should acknowledge and thank. You know who you are. I do too. It may not be good enough, but I thank you. I'll mention you by name in the next book, if there is one.

Go Red Sox.

Ed DeCosta, February 10, 2014

Your Future Self

"Plan for the future, because that's where you are going to spend the rest of your life."

– Mark Twain

Dear Reader,

Close your eyes for a moment. Take a deep breath and imagine, right now, as you read this, that you have a DVD in your hands. This is not any normal, mass produced DVD, mind you, but rather, a DVD that has a fancy inscription that reads, "Your Name – Highlights of 2018." Yes, this DVD has your name on it. And yes, it is a DVD from your future life. But roll with me on this.

For just a few minutes, suspend your disbelief and pretend that this DVD *does* exist—and that it also contains highlights of the best parts of your life in the year 2018. Got it? Okay, now take the DVD and pop it into your DVD player and hit the button marked "Play."

What do you see?

I realize that's a wide-open question. So let me give you a few specifics. The DVD you're about to watch is a professionally produced video of where you envision your life five years from now. And it's up to you to create the content on that DVD—by answering the question, "What do you want to see?"

To do that, you need to set the mood. Turn off your phone, computer, iPad, and whatever else connects you to the outside world. Maybe sink into a comfortable chair, kick off your shoes and let the experience wash over you.

We'll start with the easy stuff—the basics. It's 2018. Five years from now. What do you look like physically? Are you fatter? Thinner? How's your health? How's your energy level? Physically, how do you feel overall?

Now, let's move on to your relationships. Who are you involved with personally? Professionally? Who in your life makes you the happiest you could possibly be? And why do these people draw you in, inspire you, and motivate you? What are they like? Are they people you know right now? People you would like to know better? People you haven't met yet?

Now, keep going. What's your bank account balance? Where are you living? What do you do for a living?

Where are you spiritually? What about your family? Take a good look at everything you see. The details are important. This is your future life.

Well…at least it *can* be. That's what this book is all about—helping you *Ascend* to your future aspirations, goals, and objectives.

Ralph Waldo Emerson said, "We are born believing. A man bears beliefs as a tree bears apples." We are all equipped with the innate ability to believe and ultimately achieve amazing things in our lives.

That's why I see this DVD exercise as the perfect starting point for the journey we're about to take together.

My experience with this exercise is that my clients end up tapping into an enormous amount of emotion and personal sentiment. They connect with inner desires they might not even realize exist. They find what they *really* want in life. Five years is just long enough to feel manageable, but not so long as having the convenience of wasting time. Most of us have the ability to manifest life improvement in those five years.

So the question remains: what form do *you* want your improvements to take?

That consists of thinking past the short-term goals that distract most of us on a daily basis. You know, like organizing your desk, losing a few pounds, helping your kid pass math, and many more. They're important, and fill your time. But they may not fulfill your future goals. Your long-term goals are more *profoundly* important—and yet they're the ones that fade fast and take the back seat in the face of slightly less monumental questions such as..."Do I feel like sushi or Italian for lunch?"

Sushi's healthier, but man is Italian food good.

Seriously, though, how much time do you commit to thinking about what you're going to do with your day—as opposed to what you're going to do with your life? And there lies the value in this exercise; it motivates you to expand your horizons and allows you to look past immediate distractions to evaluate what you really want from your future-self.

And if you don't have a real vision for what you want to happen, and you don't try to develop one...well, you're just setting yourself up for failure.

It's like trying to decide between sushi and Italian for lunch and ending up with a burger. You look down and wonder how the heck you ended up with a Baconator in your hand. It wasn't what you wanted, and certainly not what you planned. It was just a by-product of maintaining no real focus.

And it's bad enough when that kind of thing just happens at lunch. It's much more diabolical if it happens when you're fifty and you wake up one day with the sudden realization that you're miserable with what you've done with both yourself and your life.

The time is now to not only clarify what you really want from life, but to begin the process of formulating a real plan to get there. You will be encouraged to separate from the routine daily demands of life and to begin to adopt the philosophy of *dreaming* bigger.

Because yes, Virginia, dreaming has value.

When you think about the great visionaries like Walt Disney, Steve Jobs, the Wright Brothers, and pretty much everyone else that has impacted our world, these people all had very strong visions of what it was they wanted to achieve. And they refused to stop or slow down until they reached their respective destinations. Now, I don't happen to have any copies of their to-do lists from back then, but it's pretty apparent these guys were driven by their dreams. It's said that in the beginning Walt Disney had this "Mickey Mouse" idea and was rejected by more than 300 banks until finally one said yes. Hence, Disneyland was born; the beginning of his dream unfolded and the rest is history.

These men were able to imagine things that didn't yet exist—things just like your future life. And they were able to bring them to life, even though a whole lot of other people told them that they couldn't do it, and even if they did, it wouldn't make a real difference.

Now, you might be saying, "Wait a minute. My aspirations do not consist of creating the next best computer, or a large theme park, or reinventing methods of travel. All I want to do is improve my life."

But what if I told you it is not about changing the world, it is about improving yours? It's not about you creating these world-changing events in your life, but instead, it's about creating a plan allowing these little miracles to unfold. Because before they were great achievers, those innovators, those creators, those men and women who generate earth-shattering breakthroughs—they were all great *believers*. What if that level of belief, that power to dream and then make dreams come true, was the common thread that allowed these great men and women to reach those heights, and to break through the limiting beliefs of others and change the world?

Your belief makes your dream a part of your very being and motivates you to make a tremendous effort over a long period of time—since there's no "overnight success" aspect to any of this. Success is, of course, a journey, not a destination. But it only becomes part of the journey when you choose to maintain a high level of effort and focus in your life. And it all begins with that powerful dream that propels you forward.

Dream, belief, and achievement are the order in which these powerful principles enter your life. So when I ask, "What do you see?" it's because everything starts with your vision for your future.

Even if you only see something in your imagination, if you visualize it vividly, you have a much easier time believing it can come true. Of course, the catch-22 here is that once you believe in it, you have an easier time *seeing* it. That's just one of the great ironies of the human condition, but it does hold true for most people.

So put down that Baconator if you're still holding one and check out that DVD of yours. See where you want to be in 2018...or five years from whenever you're reading this.

And then, read on and let me help you get there.

All the best,

Ed

PART I:

BASE CAMP

"A successful man is one who can lay a firm foundation with the bricks others have thrown at him."

- David Brinkley

"I cannot teach anybody anything. I can only make them think."

- Socrates

"Start every day off with a smile and get it over with."

- W. C. Fields

Chapter One:

What Do You Want?

What do you want?

Everything that follows in your life springs from your ability to answer that question as honestly and completely as possible. It requires a whole truckload of thought on your part—because it's easy to get confused by that question, even though it seems pretty simple and straightforward. One of the reasons for that is that there are probably a lot of people around you who think they can answer that question for you.

But, let's get real; only *you* know the answer. And sometimes, not even you. A lot of the time, what you *think* you want is just an illusion and stands in the place of what you really want.

I have a friend who was once on the verge of massive success. Everything he dreamed of was about to come his way—and in a big way; it was kind of like he bought a ticket in the career lottery and hit the jackpot.

Then he started seeing a vision. No, he didn't see the Virgin Mary on a can of Coke Zero or anything that wacky…but what he did see in his mind was his future life. He saw himself in a giant mansion, the place his new success might take him. But the mansion felt cold and empty. It made *him* feel cold and empty.

That vision brought him to the realization that everything he worked towards in his life wasn't delivering the happiness he imagined it would. His subconscious was letting him know that other things in his life, negative things, would keep him emotionally stale and in the same place as he was before the success. But even worse, he quickly understood that the success itself wasn't going to change how he felt about his life.

Quickly, he made some hard, painful choices—and today, he's not in a mansion, but he's doing well and he's a whole lot happier than he would have been otherwise.

However, the value in this story is not the fact that he changed his mind and decided to go in a different direction. The real takeaway is how he came to this difficult conclusion. This guy's brain popped in its own "DVD of the future." And when he got a good look at it, he didn't see what he expected at all. He was surprised, but more than anything, he was horrified.

And rather than completely shutting down and turning off the DVD, he was open-minded and realized what he really wanted in his life.

My friend was not alone in being confused. Many people think reaching a certain goal will instantly solve their problems and present the happiness for which they're searching. That goal could be as big as making a million dollars or something more meaningful like getting married and building a family. It could be as small as buying a beautiful car or going on a nice vacation.

Everyone deserves happiness—but how many actually obtain it? We all have the ability to achieve a high level of satisfaction with who we are, who we're with and what we're doing. It is just a matter of recognizing how.

To do that, you have to find the right answer to the question, "What do I want?" And to do that, you must work from the inside out.

A million dollars isn't going to make you happy if your day-to-day life still doesn't fulfill you. A marriage isn't going to make you happy if it's to the wrong person. And a vacation will provide only temporary relief if you return to the same job that overworks you and under satisfies you. These are only external fixes—like putting a Band-Aid on a broken arm or pulling a shade down over a cracked window.

The reality is that happiness is about connecting with your inner purpose and living according to that purpose in order to become the best possible version of you. And when you connect with that inner purpose, you are able to best determine what you want.

Believing Like a Child

Sometimes making that connection means you have to stop being an adult for a few minutes. Why? Because we get conditioned as we enter adulthood to think in certain patterns. As I mentioned earlier, we get told, over and over again, what we should want—by our parents, by our siblings, by our teachers, by our friends and partners, by societal conventions, by our bosses, even by (or maybe in particular by) the bombardment of all forms of media.

I mean, c'mon, what would you do for a Klondike Bar? Hopefully just go to a store and purchase a box. Nothing more.

That's a lot of noise—and that noise can easily drown out what our inner beliefs are trying to tell us. It was different when you were a kid, because your heart and soul were yelling too loudly to let anyone else get in the way. You ever hear a four year-old negotiate with Mom or Dad for something they REALLY want? Now that's somebody who knows what they want and isn't afraid to let the whole world know about it. And isn't it swell when they're screaming for a candy bar in a supermarket full of people? Nope, not embarrassing at all. Talk about guerrilla negotiation skills.

But just imagine if you went after what you wanted as an adult with that same level of passion (and, okay, maybe a little less volume). Imagine if you didn't stop until you got what you wanted. Think about having the ability to drown out the naysayers and move forward in a manner that is fully and completely dedicated to achieving dreams and manifesting goals.

When you connect to your inner child, you connect to your real passion. You allow yourself to see possibilities your adult self would think were impossible. You ask questions that you ordinarily might think were too uncomfortable to explore, and you find the courage to plan how to get what you want, even if it means facing some pretty high-level fear.

On a recent family vacation, I watched my three children, their cousins and friends agonize over going on an amusement park ride that they were all, frankly, scared to death to try. All eight of them finally did it anyway—even though they continued to be terrified while they were on the ride.

But when they got off…there were a lot of smiles. They were delighted by the result.

Now, they never would have experienced that joy if they didn't overcome their initial fear. That is the power of the inner child. It is the ability to recognize your fear and then deal with it.

Kids don't like rules. They don't like structure. They like to be free to be who they are. We may not be able to enjoy that kind of freedom 24/7 in the 9 to 5 world, but we need to access that way of thinking when we're trying to define our goals. We can't know what we truly want if we're cutting off 99% of the potential paths with such standard mental roadblocks such as, "That's too impractical," "I'm too young/old to take that on" or "That would be way too much trouble."

On the other hand, kids can fly through space, transform into a superhero or become a beautiful princess. They instantly snap into their own personal fantasyland whenever they want, making everything possible. They live in the moment and have an uncharacteristic love for what the future holds.

Why should they have all the fun?

When it comes to defining what you want, you have to open your mind to everything, until you hit on what inspires you *and* encompasses what you like to do. It is about finding what you are good at, and what's going to bring you satisfaction in your life and work.

When you find that purpose, you may look at it the same way my kids eyed that amusement park ride and say to yourself, "I can't get on that ride. That's way too scary!"

I'm not disagreeing with the last part. Change can bring on the feeling of fear—but you can still get on that ride and enjoy it. One of the reasons my kids could do it was because they saw lots of people getting off the ride who looked like they had the thrill of their lives (I won't talk about the ones who looked a little green around the gills).

Do the same with your dreams. Look at others who have done what you want to do. Examine how they accomplished that goal, whatever it might be, and use that information to understand how it's possible for you to do it—and, most importantly, reassure yourself that it is possible. Don't be the kid sitting on the sidelines because you are too fearful to take the chance.

So, once again, I ask you…what do you want?

What are you asking for from life? What are you doing to make it happen? There's an inner child in you, waiting to experience your life to its fullest potential. Are you ready to unlock it?

Listen to that voice.

Don't drown it out with the practicality of the grown-up voices that crowd your thinking. Go do it, and by all means, have fun doing it!

Chapter Two:

Think Big! (Or Stay Small)

What would you attempt if you knew you could not fail?

I want you to take a moment to really think about it, just like you did with the DVD exercise in this book's forward. This is a big idea. So it calls for really big and exciting thoughts.

I coach high achievers, company presidents, college deans, self-made millionaires and lots of entrepreneurs and executives. They vary by age, gender, faith, political views, fitness and relationship status—but one thing they have in common is this: they are humungous thinkers.

They also have another thing in common. Many of these people reject the notion of failure altogether. Instead, they like to call it "Temporarily Undesirable Results."

Sure, you can call it a mind game. But that, my friend, is precisely the point. Your mind is a very powerful instrument. The more you train it to work for you, instead of against you, the more successful you will be. So let's refer to it as a vantage point. It is an attitude and a way to view life.

The successful people I coach have all achieved, or are achieving, big results because their success triangle was inverted. At the base was thinking big, and as they gained success, then they filled in the small details. As you embark on this journey to reach a higher level in your own life, it is time to ask yourself, "Am I thinking big?" Or if you are thinking big, ask yourself, "Am I thinking big enough?"

If you're like most people, you're not really thinking big. Most people are stuck in small-mindedness, limiting themselves to that which is realistic, doable, practical or some other self-limiting word. They like to live in the world of "ordinary" rather than "amazing." It's not that we start out that way. Remember, in the last chapter, when we talked about everything we could become instantly in our heads when we were kids? Before you transform yourself into, say, a fairy princess or astronaut or cowboy, you don't first ask yourself if that's realistic, doable and practical. You simply take the plunge and enjoy the process.

But somewhere along the line, we are told that "growing up" means letting go of "childish things" and that daydreaming is for losers. And way, way too many of us classify dreams, whether they're in the day or night, as silly and immature instead of what they really are—relentless motivators.

With this notion in mind, if you truly desire to achieve great results, you must drop your resistance to big ideas. And there is no time like the present. Every day that goes by with you leading with limiting beliefs is nothing more than a lost opportunity to achieve an unbelievable result because as long as you think small, you will not see big results, no matter how hard you work. New York Times best selling author H. Jackson Brown Jr. of *Life's Little Instruction Book* put it this way: *"Think big thoughts, but relish small pleasures."* As you think beyond your comfort zone, consider the potential that lies within you. It's right there. Reflect on your life and evaluate some of your accomplishments and challenges that you have overcome. With these in mind, consider your thought process when beginning your personal journey to achieve these goals. Now capture those moments and store them for future use. This train of thought is what separates the big dreams from the small ones. The fight, the relentless drive, the ability to drown out the noise, the desire to prove everyone wrong and make a huge difference in both your life and the lives of others are the qualities that turn little dreamers into big ones.

Maybe you'll never actually become that fairy princess or astronaut or cowboy. But you have no idea what you will find, or how far you can go, if you let yourself think big.

It reminds me of a term I learned a few months ago. My teenage daughter Laura and my wife Linda both found it completely hilarious that I was unfamiliar with the term "YOLO."

According to the women in my life, all but nine of the 7+ billion people on the planet already know what YOLO's all about, so the odds are that none of the other eight laggards are reading this book. Sadly, I stand alone.

So, you probably know YOLO. Now that I know YOLO, I love YOLO. Yes, some college students use YOLO to justify irresponsible, reckless behavior. But to me, it stands for the fundamental concept presented in this book.

You. Only. Live. Once.

How true is that? You only get one life. So what are the implications? There are too many to list, but here are a few to get you thinking...

Give life everything you have.

Go "all in all the time."

Don't waste precious moments.

Turn off the television and take time to disconnect.

Forgive people. Yes, even him or her.

Live harder.

Love more.

Laugh easily.

Teach your children.

Give to others.

Make a bucket list.

Thank your parents or others who deserve gratitude.

Play big, 'cause playing small sucks.

Create a gratitude list.

Which takes me back to the beginning of this chapter. Most importantly, think Big. If you only get one life, as YOLO so wisely reminds us all, why on earth would you want that life to be small, limited, and anything less than the amazing life that's waiting for you if you just go for it?

Consider the question: what would you do if you knew you could not fail? Reflect on those super-successful people, who believe there is no such thing as failure; there are just Temporarily Undesirable Results.

Now go for it. The world is waiting for you.

Oliver Wendell Holmes once said, *"Man's mind, stretched to a new idea, never goes back to its original dimension."*

A group of kids were asked about their purpose in life. They responded that they wanted to become CEO's of companies; or become successful entrepreneurs; or run multi-national corporations. You get the picture. Now, they were hypothetically given $10M, and then asked about their purpose in life. Their answer changed to doing things that were much more philanthropic, all while thinking big. They found their real purpose, as they weren't hindered by the restraints of monetary constriction.

Your life will become so powerful and fulfilling when you combine finding your true purpose and stretching your mind to think big. When you accomplish that you will never think small again.

YOLO.

Chapter Three:

Don't Just Sit There – SIZZLE!

We are judged by the company we keep. You've heard this from an early age and it carries an enormous amount of value in today's world. I was always told, "When you hang out with dogs, you catch fleas." But lets take a moment and evaluate the flipside to this equation. The company you keep may define you, but you and your actions will also define your company.

So the question becomes, what are you putting out there for others to see, and what do your actions, thoughts, behavior, and decisions bring back? What kind of people are comfortable soaring with you in your orbit? Negative personalities who feel they've found a like-minded soul? Or those positive achievers who get jazzed by your energy?

When it comes to attracting the right kind of people, I liken it to fishing. The goal is to spear fish, not net fish. We don't want to throw out a big net into the ocean and pull it up to only find a couple of fish but mostly rocks, seaweed, and other ocean debris. Rather, fish with a spear; target your catch and ensure you don't attract the bottom feeders for which you have no need. The same is true when it comes to friendship and building relationships. The goal is quality over quantity. And it all starts with a fundamental understanding of how you are perceived.

Understanding how you're perceived helps you understand yourself. You may be totally unaware of how negative—or how positive—you come across to both strangers and friends.

So let's start with some self-reflection. To begin to understand the image you project to the outside world, talking to some people you trust will provide honest feedback. Look for a consensus on qualities that a few people mention. What you'll learn may be a pleasant surprise—or a disappointing realization. Most likely, it will be a mixture of the two. Either way, there is benefit to the exercise.

Knowledge is power, so it's in your best interest to understand what people think about you. Yes, you are who you are, and I'm sure there are a lot of great things about you.

But you need to find out—are those great things being projected to the world? And if so, can you do a better job of optimizing your strong qualities? This can appear as a difficult self-assessment exercise, but the rewards far outweigh the risks.

Your friends and colleagues are the very people to whom you should be talking. They know you best and can lift and inspire you to achieve at a whole new level. These are the people who can help you *Ascend*.

One way to become a magnet for those people is to deliberately create positive attitudes and self-confidence. Whether the scene is a business meeting or a cocktail party, it's an old truism that self-confidence both sells and attracts people to you. Call it swagger, call it strength, call it "knowing the score," but when you act like you've got it, other people want to get it!

I really don't mean to reduce us all to a piece of meat, but this is what it comes down to: you are the steak and self-confidence is your "sizzle."

There's a noticeable difference between a cold piece of meat that's been sitting on a plate for an hour, and a sizzling steak that's just come off a hot grill. The former can be completely unappealing, while the latter lets out an appetizing, smoky aroma that captivates even the most reluctant meat-eater. People hear it coming before they see it.

When you give yourself the sizzle that comes from self-confidence, you make yourself attractive. Your "sizzle" entices people, draws them in, and creates a magnetic affect, resulting in the desire for more people to do business with you. You will separate yourself from your competitors and find yourself positioned to grow exponentially.

But before you attempt to get that kind of sizzle going, you should tend to the steak, and build the self-confidence that acts as a precondition to make that sizzle happen. So to be clear, it all starts with one specific relationship—the relationship with the only human being who has been with you every day of your life…

YOU.

Understanding your personal relationship calls for some self-reflection and evaluation. Consider the answer to questions like:

How do you treat yourself?

Are you a harsh taskmaster, demanding perfection or other impossibilities?

Or are you closer to the other end of the spectrum, not challenging yourself to achieve what you're capable of achieving, of becoming the person you can become?

One crucial requirement to build the self-confidence that allows you to lead others, and that gives you the sizzle that attracts others, is self-leadership. The concept of self-leadership relates directly to your ability to manage and direct your own actions, decisions, and behavior. It begins by conquering your inner critic. That inner critic, a creature I like to call "the gremlin," thrives on attacking our confidence and undermining the belief that we are capable of success and happiness in life.

Gremlins want us to disapprove of ourselves and permit doubt to creep into our minds. If we allow those gremlins to hijack our minds and control our decisions, our self-esteem will eventually plummet. Since healthy self-esteem is paramount to our survival and growth, when it goes, a series of events that leads to a very dangerous state of mind occurs. In fact, self-esteem has been described as the immune system for our consciousness. It gives us strength, resilience and the capacity to overcome the very real obstacles that life inevitably presents.

So how do you develop and maintain positive self-esteem?

How do you send your own personal gremlin packing?

I'd recommend taking your gremlin to court.

No, seriously—confront your gremlin as though you two were opposing attorneys in a legal case. What evidence does it present indicating you're worthless? What logical points does it exhibit to convince an objective jury that you can't succeed? While the gremlin is good at producing sophisticated arguments, you can't trust 90% of what it has to say.

Once you've heard what the gremlin speak its piece, it's time to argue your own case. Rebutt the gremlin's line of attack with your own evidence. Consider the accomplishments to which you can point. What proven skills do you have? How have you changed people's lives in a positive manner? Enter all your supportive facts into evidence, identify those witnesses (friends and family members who know your worth) that can support your character, and don't back down until you've assembled a rock solid case. Then obliterate the inner critic in your own "mock trial."

This can be an extremely inspiriting exercise and the results should both enlighten and uplift you. Your opponent has nothing but negativity to support his position, and if you legitimately challenge him, you will undeniably prevail and save your self-esteem in the process.

Once you've gained positive self-esteem, you have to protect it. In fact, some people will tell you that maintaining self-esteem is just as difficult as obtaining it. You may feel self-confident, but how do you respond when you are challenged or questioned? It is easy to be confident when times are good. But how do you react when the going gets tough? One of the most effective tools to protect your self-esteem is through the use of positive affirmations. Some suggestions that work for me are:

My life is a beautiful, enriching experience and I am filled with awe and wonder at life's magnificence.

I am mentally and physically healthy; well-being is my natural state.

I choose to feel as good as possible at every moment of my life; even in difficult times, I remain positive, optimistic and hopeful.

The difficult times in my life are brief, quickly replaced by good times and happy moments.

Create your own daily affirmations, ones with which you're comfortable and that are applicable to your own life. These will help that gremlin of yours go down and stay down.

Positive self-esteem brings with it powerful self-confidence. And powerful self-confidence allows you to create the sizzle we talked about earlier; the sizzle that enables you to create the public impact you desire and attract the kinds of movers and shakers that can help you on your way as you *Ascend*.

Sizzling Enthusiasm

To make that sizzle happen, you need to put your self-confidence into action—and you do that by demonstrating enthusiasm.

Show enthusiasm for your product or service, regarding your experiences and about life in general. Even in the face of challenges or obstacles, it is imperative that you maintain relentless and direct enthusiasm. Everybody fails, especially those who dream big. In fact, the more you attempt, the more often you'll fall short. It's actually a badge of honor; a simple byproduct of swinging for the fences. So wear failure with pride, but don't let it define you. Failure, just like success, is experiential. It helps define the total you. Enthusiasm is a choice you make with every new endeavor, opportunity, job, or obstacle.

Especially every obstacle.

Enthusiasm is self-confidence in action. Enthusiasm drives your energy to a higher level and that energy attracts other positive people and opportunities into your life. It also helps you solve challenging problems and reach for your next goal.

You can choose to tap into that energy whenever you want, and if you do, you'll see what a difference it can make. So go ahead. Try some self-confidence on for size.

I can hear you sizzling now...

PART 2:
THE CLIMB

"Easier to climb up than to just hang on."

- Ronald Harwood

"When preparing to climb a mountain - pack a light heart."

- Dan May

"It isn't the mountains ahead to climb that wear you out; it's the pebble in your shoe."

- Muhammad Ali

Chapter Four:

Attitude and the Case for Lemonade

Lemonade has a bad rap.

Now I'm not talking about the delicious beverage that quenches your thirst in the summer sun, I'm referring to the cliché and often cited metaphor that's been planted in our heads and goes as follows: "When life gives you lemons, make lemonade."

How many times have you heard that saying? Isn't it inevitable that—after hearing it from your grandparents; after reading it on posters; after hearing it quoted on countless social media statuses and even in the news—that you might eventually feel that lemonade represents nothing but all the bad things that happen to us?

With that notion in mind, how does Minute Maid even still sell the stuff?

Lemons are those sour moments in life when we lose a business deal, when we get bad news about our health, when our teenage daughter drives the family car into the other family car, or when we, or someone close to us, makes a serious mistake that changes the landscape of our lives. Those are some serious lemons!

And lemons happen to all of us on a regular basis. They may seem to be of the smaller variety, but our lives will consist of lemons. Frankly, lemons are no big deal—just another part of life.

Except when those lemons come our way. That's when we tell a different story—and we spin that story into an epic Hollywood disaster film. Think about on how many occasions you felt your latest "lemon" was the worst thing that ever happened.

Again, put it in perspective, it was probably no big deal. It was just your turn in the Lemon Line—the cycle of life.

But your response should not be so natural. When given lemons, most people react by feeling down and out, focusing on the adverse challenges immediately presented. This natural fight or flight response often compounds the problem and prevents informed and calculated decisions. But it doesn't have to be that way. So, what should the response be to your latest lemon? Make lemonade, of course. Your grandparents were right. And Minute Maid has an awesome product. Lemonade is *good*—and good for you. When something negative happens, you haven't been given a bad break; you've been given an opportunity to demonstrate honesty, integrity, resiliency, character, resolve, composure...and even some class. Difficult times are an opportunity to demonstrate your strongest qualities. Challenges allow you to hone your skills and adapt to a complicated scenario. And obstacles promote growth and development.

Welcome the lemons, as they only build a relentless and strong character on a foundation of trust.

Good times don't provide nearly the opportunities as bad times to demonstrate these exceptional traits. Be grateful for such opportunities. They are nothing more than learning experiences and growth opportunities.

Learn to love lemonade—by learning to have a positive attitude when you receive just one lemon, or the entire lemon tree.

A positive attitude is important to your ascension. Really, your ability to climb to the top depends on it. Attitude is like an express elevator that shoots you to the top of the skyscraper of success. But that's not all it does. It can literally save your life. There are well researched and documented connections between your attitude and your health. Since the mind and body are connected, so are your health and your attitude.

Optimists live longer, happier lives because positive thinking is the natural software for your mind. Positive thinking is more than just a good idea; it's how God designed your mind to work. When we change the software, the hardware works in a different manner. It is no longer optimized, fast, and sharp. It feels clunky, dull, and no longer vibrant. So maintain a positive attitude to ensure your software is working at an extremely high level.

In the last chapter, we discussed daily affirmations to boost your self-esteem. But without a positive attitude, your efforts will generally fall short. So let's take the time to present some affirmations dedicated solely to improve your attitude as you *Ascend*:

Life delivers gifts to me daily.

I can achieve what I want.

People appreciate who I am.

I am at peace and I trust myself.

The power of these positive affirmations is remarkable, but the power of a positive attitude is life changing. It literally can move mountains. Former Major League Baseball player Wade Boggs said, "*A positive attitude causes a chain reaction of positive thoughts, events and outcomes. It is a catalyst and it sparks extraordinary results.*"

I've seen it for myself. I work with executives, am a professor at a university and have coached youth soccer for the last fifteen years. These are three distinctly different age groups and situations. But there is a common denominator that I can clearly point to as one of the driving factors for success as a leader, student, or athlete. It is the attitude of the participants.

Although these three groups are completely unique in their own light, there is a *similarity* between the three types of "players" involved: They are all attempting to reach a goal or achieve an objective. The soccer players are looking to have fun and be a part of a wonderful game. Most of the students are there to learn and obtain a valuable education, master the subject, and hopefully earn a good grade. The executives have the widest variety of goals, but they mostly relate to their personal and professional performance, their business success, and the state of their organizations.

As you can see, all three groups are all seeking success in a particular area of their lives. And they all need the right attitude to reach that pinnacle. As Thomas Jefferson said, *"Nothing can stop the man with the right mental attitude from achieving his goal; nothing on earth can help the man with the wrong mental attitude."*

Of course, there are several key variables governing whether you will be successful at any given undertaking. But the biggest piece of the pie chart in determining whether you get there or not is your attitude at the beginning. Start your journey with the right attitude and the bumps will be small. But begin with a poor attitude and you will find brick walls along your path. Whether you are a CEO with hundreds of employees or a ten-year-old learning to kick the ball properly (laces, not toes), your outlook and vantage point is the single most crucial variable in predicting your success or failure.

Consider the moving and historical journey of 1980 USA Olympic hockey team, often referred to as "The Miracle on Ice." If you're not old enough to have watched this dramatic sports story unfold, let's outline the details. This team was made up of college kids who, in order to advance to the finals, had to defeat the Soviet Red Army team, which was full of professional players who were bigger, faster and stronger than they were. The Russians had won nearly every hockey world championship and Olympic Games since 1954. By most accounts, they were considered unbeatable.

But that cheering gallery did not include Herb Brooks, the coach of Team USA. He knew that physically, his boys were completely outclassed. But he felt they did have an advantage in the mental game. If he could only impart the right attitude into his team and the belief that they could win, it was possible that the Americans could give Mother Russia a run for her money. Brooks just had to find a way to instill that passion into his team.

In the now-famous pre-game speech that has captivated the sports world, he said to his team, "This is our time! Their time is done! It's over! I'm sick and tired of hearing about what a great hockey team the Soviets have! Screw them! This is your time! Now go out there and *take it!*"

They did. In what has been considered one of the greatest upsets in sports history, Team USA advanced to the gold medal round with a 4-3 score.

Now...the question is, do you believe you can make your own miracles? If you have the right attitude, you definitely have the potential to do so.

Got a big challenge ahead of you? Facing an obstacle everyone else tells you is unbeatable? Or do you just hear the noise from the naysayers telling you that you're not good enough? Calm the noise and remember, "*Screw them! This is your time! Now go out there and take it!*"

And enjoy a nice cold glass of lemonade after you're done.

Chapter Five:

The Fear Zone: Unleashing Your Inner Lion

Courage.

We all know it when we see others demonstrate it. But what exactly *is* courage?

Well, here's one definition from the Cowardly Lion in the classic film, "The Wizard of Oz":

"Courage! What makes a king out of a slave? Courage! What makes the flag on the mast to wave? Courage! What makes the elephant charge his tusk in the misty mist, or the dusky dusk? What makes the muskrat guard his musk? Courage! What makes the Sphinx the Seventh Wonder? Courage! What makes the dawn come up like thunder? Courage!"

Or consider Nelson Mandela's definition. He learned that courage *"was not the absence of fear, but the triumph over it. The brave man is not he who does not feel afraid, but he who conquers that fear."*

Maya Angelou said, *"Courage is the most important of all the virtues, because without courage you can't practice any other virtue consistently. You can practice any virtue erratically, but nothing consistently without courage."*

But maybe these definitions are a little too loose. So let's try the etymology route and examine the word's origins. "Courage" comes from the Latin word for "heart," "cor." Courage is bravery, the willingness and ability to not only confront danger, but also overcome fear to do more, reach higher, and go bigger.

My preferred definition, however, comes from Mark Twain. He said, *"Courage is resistance to fear, mastery of fear, not absence of fear."*

In other words, courage does not replace fear—it overcomes it. Don't mistake fearlessness with courage. There are, of course, some people who apparently have little or no sense of fear. In my experience, they frequently behave recklessly. Rather than acting courageously, they foolishly place themselves and others at risk.

So just being fearless doesn't cut it. Fearlessness means you've turned off the bright red warning light attached directly to your brain that prevents you from doing things like impulsively diving into a water tank with a great white shark in it. Most people don't call that kind of fearlessness "bravery."

They refer to it as "stupidity."

That's why families, companies and teams don't need and shouldn't desire fearless fools to run the show. They need people who are courageous and smart about the risks they choose to take. Great leaders are those that recognize courage is making a difficult decision based on logical reasoning. Or standing up to a bully or negative influence on your company or those you love.

But, make no mistake; a real leader does take the right risks. I once heard a senior executive say, "Give me a team of sheep led by a lion, rather than a team of lions led by a sheep." The leader who displays courage instills courage in others. It is contagious. And besides, when lions outnumber sheep, the situation becomes more about dinner than management.

The fact is you can't grow, you can't achieve and you can't *Ascend* without some measure of courage. That's because true progress frequently involves breaking free of the things that make you feel secure and comfortable. Once you are out of your comfort zone, you can begin to grow. You will probably have to take financial, personal and/or professional risks to develop yourself and live the life you want to live. But if you don't take those risks, you stay where you are—and that's the scariest risk of them all.

And you don't want to end up looking back when you're older and examining all the chances from which you ran away. So, how do you find the courage to face your fears and take the action you need to take to reach great levels of success? Well, you begin that process by understanding that success begins with failure—and the most successful people make more mistakes than other people. It is part of the natural progression of achievement. He who has not fallen was never even on his feet in the first place. The reasons for that are obvious—successful people never stop taking those risks or trying new things, even in the face of past failure.

Frankly, it's a mistake to not make a mistake. In fact, if you're not making mistakes, you probably aren't attempting enough different things, probably because you are afraid to fail.

So think about how you can push yourself out of your comfort zone and reformat the way you approach opportunity. Consider pushing yourself into "The Fear Zone." The great thing about The Fear Zone is that it is where you feel most alive. The rush of the risk; the excitement of the challenge; the undeniable sweetness of success. Because you're not settling for the same old goal, but rather, you're reaching for a new and more exciting goal.

Those who have reached great heights of success will often reminisce about their time in The Fear Zone. They will remember it as an exhilarating and certainly necessary challenge. And the lessons they have learned from this experience should provide a valuable learning opportunity for you.

Navigating that Fear Zone with the benefit of others' experiences will help you to shrink the learning curve. Talk to people who have already accomplished what you're nervous about trying (embarking on a new career, opening a business, going back to school, moving to a new location, starting or renewing a relationship, etc…) and find out where they failed and how they eventually succeeded. Listen to their stories and allow their advice to fuel your fire. Learn from their mistakes and use them to avoid your own.

I am confident that most of these people will impart the lesson that in many situations, fear is actually your friend. For example, the fear of leaving a job incomplete or doing it poorly can be a powerful motivator to perform at your highest level. Fear can inspire you to do more, deliver more and become more.

There's a recurring theme in what people who dared to take courageous action in an important area of their lives say about their results. They usually state, "It didn't work out exactly like I thought it would...but it is still the best thing I ever did."

I think we can all live with that outcome. Better than we thought, but more difficult than we could have imagined.

As the Cowardly Lion discovered, all the courage you need is already inside you. You've just got to unleash your inner lion. Go ahead. Do it. And DO IT AFRAID.

Sheryl Sandberg, the Chief Operating Officer of Facebook put it beautifully:

"Don't let your fears overwhelm your desire. Let the barriers you face— ***and there will be barriers****—be external, not internal. Fortune does favor the bold. I promise that you will never know what you're capable of unless you try."*

So, what would you do, if only you were not afraid to try? If you weren't stuck in The Fear Zone?

A little boy at the end of the diving board is 1.2 seconds away from exhilaration and joy. We know it. His parents know it. He just doesn't know it yet. In order to know, he's got to take that fateful first step.

So now I'm talking to you. What are you afraid to try? Go ahead and jump.

Do. It. Afraid.

Chapter Six:

The Four Steps to Goal Achievement

Henry David Thoreau said, "*What you get by achieving your goals is not as important as what you become by achieving your goals.*" Everyday we wake up, we set goals. They may be life altering, or as simple as picking up the dry-cleaning. But nonetheless, our primary goal is to achieve our goals. As a coach, it's probably the most important topic we can discuss. I simply cannot overemphasize its importance. And to achieve goals at any level, you have to identify the answer to the following basic question:

How are you going to know where you're going if you don't have any destination in mind?

It might be fun for a Sunday afternoon to just point your car in a particular direction and see where you end up. But when it's your life you're talking about, random and arbitrary direction simply wont cut it. If you end up in a place where you *don't* want to be, it's a lot more difficult and time-consuming to do a U-turn. In fact, the biggest mistake we can make is not failing to reach our goals, but expending valuable time to reach goals we never really wanted in the first place.

So set goals. Not just in your head. Write them down. And take directed steps to achieve them every single day.

But most importantly, make them S-M-A-R-T. S-M-A-R-T stands for:

Specific

Measurable

Attainable

Relevant

Time-bound

Let's look at each of those words to determine how they relate to our overall goals.

Specific. That's pretty easy. Maybe your goal is to be successful. But how do you define success? How will success look for you? The point is that your goal to be successful is great. But how you will define success is even more important.

Measurable. How are you going to measure your success? You can't just say, "Well, I'll be good at something," and let it go at that. For example, if you define success as booking thirty speaking engagements per year, you now have a quantifiable and measurable goal. In fact, you can project whether or not you will meet your goals on a monthly basis. You can measure and certainly evaluate if you are doing a good job or if you need to alter your actions to put yourself in a better position to succeed.

Attainable. Okay, hang on…can you really expect to become the greatest speaker in the world? Setting unattainable goals is just as bad as not setting goals in the first place. Consider a potentially realistic goal and shoot a little higher. That way you'll remain driven but also put yourself in a position where you can actually succeed. You don't want it to take a miracle to reach your goals.

Relevant. Relevance can be tricky, but there are some questions you can ask yourself to establish it—questions such as, "Is this goal worthwhile?" "Is it really in line with the rest of my needs and wants?" "Am I actually capable of becoming a successful speaker?" And, "Is this the right time in my life to put so much effort into speaking?" The concept of relevance falls on the notion that the goal you have set is actually one that will better your life and fulfill your needs. If your goal is to become a credible speaker, but you are a chef from 9-5, you may be investing time in an irrelevant goal. The point is that when setting your goals; consider how they relate to the other important parts of your life. And if they do not, then it is time to reassess.

Time-bound. When it comes to achieving goals, time is of the essence. A goal without a timeline is nothing more than a dream. And while dreaming is important, it can actually be an impediment or crutch when striving to achieve goals. When setting goals, simultaneously set time-frames for achieving those goals. Otherwise, you will find yourself making excuses and prolonging the process.

But, frankly, going through the whole SMART process still might not mean anything if you are not dedicated and determined to reaching your goals. Some people see the process of setting goals as a goal in of itself—and never actually follow through on reaching those goals. Of course, the real purpose of setting goals is achieving them. Otherwise... what's the point?

Which brings me to the Four Steps for the Achievement of Goals.

Here are four steps to consider if you find yourself regularly falling short of your goals:

STEP 1: Set SMART goals, as we just discussed. Make sure ALL letters are represented. You don't want a SART goal or a SMRT goal or even a SMAR goal. When you make sure your goals are SMART, you'll find that they are realistic objectives that can actually be measured and eventually reached. When they're not SMART, they're frequently not realistic enough to even be feasible.

STEP 2: Visualize achieving a goal and **tap into the feelings** that you'll experience when you reach it. Does achieving that goal make you happy? Proud? Or frustrated and dissatisfied? Who will care and why?

What gets better when you achieve the goal? Be as clear as possible about the emotions you not only want to experience, but also will experience. Close your eyes and imagine them as vividly as possible. This technique is called guided imagery. Why? Making your goals SMART was more of an intellectual exercise. Visualizing this is more about your heart and soul—your feelings. If they're not fully invested in your goal, you may lose motivation and focus in your efforts.

STEP 3: Identify and analyze **the obstacles that might stand in the way** of your goal. People? Places? Your own negative thoughts? Lack of funds? Time? Or procrastination?

Write those obstacles down and visualize what they might look like as people (unless they already *are* people, of course). Now...imagine they're all heckling you. Mocking you. Trying to intimidate you by talking about how they're going to *STOP YOU.*

"You think you actually have time to do all that?"

"You're going to lose all that weight?"

"Are you sure that is not just a really bad idea?"

STEP 4: Fight back—and create viable strategies to take on the doubters, haters, and naysayers. This usually calls for you to understand how you're going to deal with the obstacles in advance. Write down the strategies you come up with and have them firmly implanted in your head. When the doubters, haters and naysayers make themselves known (and they will), you'll know exactly how to overcome them and move forward. However, if you're unprepared for the opposition, you leave yourself open to defeat.

I don't want you to get beaten. I want to see you become the best at what you choose to do. I want to look up in the sky and watch you *Ascend* to unbelievably great heights.

Chapter Seven:

The Project Is...YOU! Planning Out Your "Elephant Bites"

In the last chapter, we talked about setting goals. It's important to have your destination in mind whenever you're trying to create meaningful and profound change in your life.

Of course, it doesn't do much good to have that destination figured out...*if you have no idea how you're going to get there.* It's kind of like trying to take a road trip without a car. In my experience, walking can take a lot longer.

So what's the "vehicle" that's going to take you where you want to go? Is it education? A mentor or a coach? Or just good old-fashioned hard work?

I wouldn't doubt that your vehicle ends up being a hybrid, which is a combination of a few different, but important, elements. And I also wouldn't doubt you're going to have to put some firm plans in place to decide how to juggle those elements and prioritize how you will use them. If it's a substantial goal, it's going to require that you make some pivotal changes in yourself. As the 19th century Irish poet Oscar Wilde said, *"The aim of life is self-development. To realize one's nature perfectly—that is what each of us is here for."*

Our external progress is heavily linked to our internal process. If we want to have love, happiness and success, we have to prepare our heart and soul to enable those good things to happen. The principles of personal development are easily accessible to us all and the process is pretty straightforward.

Again, it begins with the goal you have in mind—and then determining how you're going to reach that goal. Your starting point should be to clearly *visualize* what that goal means to you.

If you don't feel like you have a crystal-clear, burning desire to achieve that goal, don't let *that* stop you either. Humans are tricky creatures. We can talk ourselves out of anything that seems hard or challenging. But what we may really be talking ourselves out of is real happiness. We can't just be human beings taking the easy road. We have to become "human doings," taking the road less traveled and the facing challenges it presents. Only until we face that truth about ourselves can we find real happiness.

Change is difficult to accept. Change is also inevitable, and we have to learn to manage all our affairs at the speed of change. Remember the law of inertia—it takes a lot to move a rock just like it takes a lot more to make us get up off our butts. It's important to initiate movement, because sometimes (in fact very often), we end up learning what we need to do *by trying to do it.*

So reflect, meditate, and pray on what you'd like to change in your life—physically, emotionally, intellectually, spiritually, and financially. Look specifically at the area of your life that you know is in need of some kind of transformation. It may be your family relationships, your love life, or your career. If there's more than one area, then consider how those areas might be linked by your overall approach to situations and relationships.

Then, begin to plan how to reach your desired destination. Map out a series of steps and a set of specific actions. Set milestones you need to achieve. But most importantly, attach deadlines and timetables to those milestones. Putting expiration dates on action steps is a vital mental tool that pays big dividends.

When you think that you have forever to make a change, you'll end up *taking* forever. And, in this case, "forever" usually means "*never.*"

Creating significant change almost always seems like an overwhelming endeavor—kind of like trying to eat an elephant. We can both agree it's easy to walk away from that kind of challenge.

But there's an old riddle that goes like this:

Q: How do you eat an elephant?

A: One bite at a time.

The day you start your journey is the day you begin meeting that challenge. It's also the day you start getting closer to conquering it. You are your ultimate project. And there's no better day to get started on that project than today.

Here are a few "elephant bites" to help you plan and succeed in that project:

ELEPHANT BITE #1: Find an ACCOUNTABILITY PARTNER

Choose someone close to you that knows you well and is trustworthy. Then, tell that person your goal and give them permission to regularly check in on your progress. When you know there is accountability, it can heighten your motivation and follow-through. When it's just you monitoring yourself, you'll inevitably end up looking the other way.

ELEPHANT BITE #2: Use a TIME TRACKING TOOL

It could be the big calendar your insurance agent sent you last Christmas that's hanging on the wall. It could be Microsoft Outlook. It could be any kind of time/task software you have on your tablet, laptop or smart phone. Whatever you decide to use, make sure you schedule your timetables and deadlines and then refer to it *every single day* to ensure you're staying on the right track.

ELEPHANT BITE #3: DOCUMENT your Progress

When you document your progress, you can see how far you've come and get a sense of real accomplishment that will help you move forward and motivate you to *Ascend* toward your ultimate goal. At the very least, log the basic facts of your accomplishments on a day-to-day basis. Ideally, write a couple paragraphs—a thought log—of how you feel and where you are at that time. A more detailed journal will help you keep in touch with your evolving self.

ELEPHANT BITE #4: ANTICIPATE Problems and Setbacks

We talked about this in the last chapter. If you're not prepared for what can go wrong with your plan, you're not prepared to be proactive in dealing with complications. As the old saying goes, "Hope for the best, but expect the worst."

Or as the Boy Scout motto says, "Be Prepared!"

Keep all these elephant bites in mind as you move forward and you'll finally get to the point where you're looking at nothing but elephant bones.

But rest assured I practice what I preach. Recently, I decided it was the optimal time to pursue my lifelong dream of playing music. The first step of my plan was to talk to my friend who gives guitar lessons. We discussed my goal, I bought a guitar, we set up weekly lessons and homework, and I granted him permission to endlessly ridicule me if I quit. My first real deadline was to play a recognizable James Taylor song for my family at Christmas. What I didn't anticipate was my fingers getting so sore in the process! Yes, I've got pain in my fingers, but part of me is happy to feel it—because it's a reminder that I'm finally working towards something I've always wanted to do. For that pay-off, I can deal with a little "Fire and Rain," right?

The project is You.

The time is now.

What are you waiting for?

Chapter Eight:

Setting Priorities, or, Can a Ninja Beat a Vampire?

At this point, we can agree that planning is important. However, we must simultaneously take into consideration a pretty good law that a fellow with the last name of Murphy came up with many, many years ago. You've probably heard it: *Whatever can go wrong, will go wrong.*

Murphy's Law has taught us the world does not always turn precisely the way we'd like it to. While planning is important, it is not going to insulate you from unexpected events beyond your control.

So while planning should always remain a priority, it should be accompanied by *priorities.* Priorities allow you to maintain your focus, shield you from distractions, protect yourself from stress and, occasionally, avoid complete and utter disaster. But they're not set in stone; circumstances can quickly turn them upside down.

For example, how important are eating and drinking to your daily life? I'd think they fall pretty high on your priority list. But what if you suddenly can't breathe? How important are food and water now? Probably a little less important than the oxygen you need to survive. The point is that a more urgent and sudden priority can quickly relegate your number one priority to the back burner.

Recently, I experienced a similar scenario. I went to sleep with a pretty normal plan in my head for the next day. I planned to attend a few meetings, make a couple of phone calls, go work out, and even write a chapter for this book.

Well, when I awoke, I found two of my family members were really sick. Obviously, my work went by the wayside because my *life* priorities dictated that I implement a "Plan B" for the day. I did that without regret, disappointment or guilt—I simply welcomed my true priorities. I found that it was actually an opportunity to show my love in action, Sixteen hours later, my "patients" were on the road to recovery and I returned to my "normal schedule."

An emergency like that doesn't happen every day. More often, we're just trying to sort out all of our so-called "normal" stuff. These consist of the day-to-day decisions and priorities like the little unimportant tasks that often distract us from the big ones. We end up stumbling from one thing to another, never finishing anything and never feeling any sense of accomplishment.

Many of my coaching clients have difficulty with time management, and they often ask me for the secret to what makes a person truly productive. The key is contained in the following phrase:

"Plan Your Work, Work Your Plan."

Let's start with the first half of that directive. When you "plan your work," you create a schedule for any given time period, guided by your highest priorities and your overall purpose. Always keep in mind that there can be no productivity without *priorities*, just as there can be no real priorities without *purpose*.

Planning your work involves scheduling meetings on your calendar and then preparing for those same meetings. It also includes locating time for recreation, for your family, for exercise, for faith, for reading, and even time for simple, quiet reflection. Each of these should be viewed as an appointment and scheduled in the same manner that you would a trip to the dentist or conference call. They are imperative to your mental and physical health as they help you create a balanced and healthy life. If everything doesn't fit, you should just start cutting from the bottom of your list of priorities, shortening commitments, and even eliminating meetings that are not absolutely necessary.

With that in mind, let's discuss the second half of the quote "Plan your work, work your plan". When you "work your plan," you need to tap into the qualities of *responsibility* and *discipline,* as these twin towers of strength enable you to truly commit to success and reaching your highest potential. Responsibility and discipline make you virtually *immune to distraction,* because they provide you with a single-minded focus on where you're going and what you have to do to get there.

That's productivity in action. But let's get back to that list of priorities. For the list to actually help you achieve productivity, it has to be properly arranged. And for that to happen, you should create a hierarchy of priorities.

We all end up with a lot of responsibilities on our plates during our day-to-day lives. Another distraction is always lurking around the corner, no matter how organized you are.

The good news is you can manage these unexpected bumps in the road by transforming yourself into a Ninja. When a Ninja has five attackers headed in his direction, he knows who to take out first, second, third, fourth and fifth. If he didn't know how to figure out the right sequence of takedowns, he'd have to find a new occupation.

As an executive coach, I often deal with clients who face multiple "attackers" each day—a deadline on a big project gets moved up, a key member of the staff announces their departure, or a big order gets cancelled. They get confused about what to do and when to do it.

We all do. It is in our nature and a part of life. In our professional and personal lives, we are often required to make tough choices about what we're going to do with our time. That's when it's good to heed the words of Dr. Stephen Covey, the author of *The Seven Habits of Highly Effective People:*

"The key is <u>not</u> to prioritize what's on your schedule, but to schedule <u>your</u> priorities."

Here's how I like to determine my priorities. First, I start with a list of my highest goals, those things I consider most important in my world.

For me, it goes like this: faith, love, family, fitness, business, finances, personal development, and fun. If a demand doesn't relate to one of these big rocks, I devote absolutely no time to it.

Secondly, I utilize a method that prioritizes tasks for my schedule. I call it the C-A-T method. This acronym includes:

Criticality: How important is this task to my overall goals and purpose?

Actionability: Do I have the information and resources necessary to complete the task? Or should I wait until more resources are available?

Time: How much time will this task take? What's the deadline for getting it done? Do I have enough time today to make adequate progress on it?

I then rate each of the tasks on a scale from one to ten, based on the C-A-T acronym. Next, I rearrange the list from highest (thirty points) to lowest (three points) and sequentially place them into my schedule. I know I am done when my schedule is fully booked.

Any task that did not make the cut simply does not get done.

This process will genuinely help you reflect on your priorities. You will get the things done that you most need and want to get done, and rarely will allow yourself to be victimized by needless tasks.

This technique has proven to be enormously valuable in maximizing my productivity. I instantly become a Ninja, slicing and dicing every task that comes my way with remarkable efficiency.

Unless someone in my family comes down with a fever. Then I simply put my sword away for the day and put some chicken soup on the stove.

After all, you have to have your priorities.

Chapter Nine:

Choices: The Calendar and the Checkbook

Now that we are on the same page regarding how to prioritize, let's shift our focus to discussing how to put priorities into action.

This starts with the *choices* we make in our everyday lives.

When you endeavor to *Ascend*, you'll be making plenty of those choices along the way. Those choices will either take you to a higher place or bring you down.

You may think you have your priorities in place. But as the saying goes, actions speak louder than words. Those actions take form in many ways; like how you live, how you speak, how much respect you show to others, and how much respect you show to yourself. The choices you make demonstrate the values you *really* hold, despite what you might tell yourself.

That's why it's important to really take a look at those choices and what they both imply and represent about the type of person you are. The way in which you can do that is through utilizing two common and critical everyday "measurement tools." Your *calendar* and your *checkbook*.

Let's start with your calendar. Whether it's the one you use on your smart phone or the one you hang on your wall, you most likely have a calendar you regularly consult for scheduling purposes.

Instead of looking forward to future dates, for once, I'd like you to take a look back. Try to remember what you did on each day of the past week or even month. This will help you visualize the choices you make with regard to your time—time you will never get back.

Make a list of all the activities you engaged in during your waking hours and then break them down into categories like those we mentioned above, notating how much time you spent in each category. If you're really ambitious about this, you can even create a pie chart to see how your time is spent.

So—how did this exercise turn out for you? Did you read a good book in your spare time? Did you try to educate yourself or expand your capabilities in some way? Did you spend time interacting with your loved ones in a real and meaningful way?

Or did you spend hours flipping back and forth between a few of those 500 satellite channels you have at your fingertips?

Don't get me wrong, everybody needs to relax. But when chill time puts a chill on every other aspect of your life, you may want to re-evaluate why you're making these choices.

This isn't about time management, this is about *choice* management. Your choices are either governed by your *professed priorities* and values or they're governed by what you simply feel like doing at any given moment, with little regard to your clearly defined priorities.

Are you making active choices or passive ones? Either way, it's your choice.

Now, let's move on to the checkbook. You're probably aware of the often-cited statistic that the number one topic married couples fight about is money.

That's because money, like time, is a finite resource. When we use it up on silly or unnecessary spending, we don't have enough for what could be important and even life changing necessities. And when two people share that money, and one doesn't agree with what the other is doing with it, things can get pretty complicated.

So let's do the same thing we did with the calendar. Look back on your expenditures for the past month. If you use Quicken or another financial program, it can probably generate its own instant pie chart to give you a better understanding of what you're doing with your dough.

Again, break down the money you spent into categories of expenditures. And look at where you're investing your hard-earned dollars.

If you haven't done this before, you may be surprised—or possibly even shocked—at the results. Don't be. Most people spend the money, but rarely track their spending decisions. In my experience, most people spend more than they realize on small things like comfort food, cable television and clothes that they don't need. Even worse, the big things like charities, faith, physical fitness and personal development get lost in the money shuffle.

What expenditures do you make that you regret? How can you improve your financial choices so you feel good about them and they reflect your desired priorities?

When it comes to what you say you care about, do you put your money where your mouth is?

It's not that much fun to audit yourself. But, that's what my calendar and checkbook exercises force you to do. It's uncomfortable, but necessary, to shine a light on yourself. You're reviewing the choices you made with time and money and determining if those choices are justified against your professed priorities.

But you don't have to stop there (even though you probably want to). You can do this with any aspect of your life that you feel needs this kind of "self-audit." It could be the food you eat, the books you read, or the exercise you're getting (or *not* getting).

We all make hundreds, even thousands, of choices every week in all sizes shapes and forms. How aware are you of what those choices mean about you when you make them? How much thought or effort do you put into making sure the choices are healthy ones that will help you *Ascend*? You probably just make them and then move on.

Review your priorities and review your choices. If they're dangerously misaligned, change one or the other.

Choose whether to *Ascend* – or to stay earthbound.

Chapter Ten:

Create a New Comfort Zone (With Help from Seinfeld, The Simpsons and Matt Damon)

There's an intense scene in the movie *Good Will Hunting* where Minnie Driver's character, Skylar, asks Will Hunting (played by Matt Damon) to come to California with her.

"I can't," he says, "because I live here."

Will Hunting can't leave his "comfort zone." Meaning, he will not only miss out on the love of Skylar, but also Disneyland, Malibu Beach and meeting Brad Pitt and George Clooney.

Psychologists teach us that a "comfort zone" is an artificial mental boundary within which you maintain a sense of security, and *out* of which you experience great discomfort. Of course, while these boundaries may be artificial in the eyes of the world's psychological professionals, they can be pretty real to you and me.

We create comfort zones because they provide exactly what they advertise—comfort. It's where we feel like we are "Masters of Our Domain." We feel like we're in control, on top of whatever might be going on, and maybe most importantly, like nothing particularly strange or threatening could possibly occur.

And therein lies the problem.

Sure, your comfort zone may be…well, comfortable. But it may also be so small that it prevents you from *living the life you desire*. It may actually serve as a barrier between you and those achievements you want more than anything else—in your career, in your social life, with your health, and with your finances.

So you probably already know what I'm going to say next: You've got to expand your comfort zone in order to grow.

However, that can be easier said than done for most people. Expanding your comfort zone can be, as you might expect, *uncomfortable*.

That's because challenging situations can trigger negative thoughts, and those thoughts prevent us from performing at our best. We plant seeds of doubt that create these self-induced barriers to success. We then retreat, seeking safety, and get even *more* comfortable within those barriers. We pop some popcorn, plop down in our favorite chair and watch that *Seinfeld* rerun. Or six or seven *Seinfeld* reruns. Or maybe a few *Simpsons* reruns.

I remember one where Homer's dad and all the other residents were suddenly released from their old age home. They ran outside, feeling empowered by their newfound freedom, cheering themselves on in their new lives. But then they suddenly stopped and looked around with wary eyes, and Grandpa Simpson said, "I don't like the look of those teenagers." They all quickly hurried back *inside*.

That's just the thought process to which I am referring. When you first get the guts to break out of your comfort zone, you feel an initial rush of excitement from pushing the envelope and heading in a direction you may have never been before. Then you get a good look at your new environment, realize you have no idea where you are or what to do next, and you run for cover. Or at least return to a place you find to be comfortable.

While this is a natural human impulse, it is also a *limiting* one. But this doesn't have to be your reaction. You can change your world by shifting your perspective.

Your comfort zone is actually a reflection of your self-image—how you think and feel about yourself and how you expect things should appear and feel. So in order to expand your comfort zone, *you need to expand your self-image.*

To do that, you must first rid yourself of the self-judgment, self-doubt, and self-limiting beliefs that keep you trapped in your psychic cave.

So where do you start? Begin with the small things and go from there.

- Focus on what you want, not on how to get it.
- Make a promise to yourself to try.
- Expect difficulty and welcome it. Pain is required, but misery is optional.
- Create a new cycle, one full of increasing successes and confidence.

By taking these steps, you will ultimately create a whole new comfort zone.

And the end result? Once you feel really good about yourself, it's easy to step outside of your old comfort zone and into a more exciting place within your life. So, build your confidence and self-respect first, *and then* step out.

You will discover that you are larger than the challenges in your life. And that the truth is, your security and happiness does not reside in anything or anyone outside of you. Rather, it lies solely *within* you.

Once you make the decision to move beyond the circumstances, people, and experiences with which you are familiar, you manifest personal growth. It is a path that forces you to stretch yourself, destroy your supposed limits and become more than you were before.

Recently, Neil Armstrong, the great astronaut and the first man to walk on the moon, passed away. Talk about getting out of your comfort zone—being the first man on the moon is pretty far out!

Armstrong would never have ascended out of our galaxy if he wasn't willing to risk it all, just so he could take that giant leap.

If you're willing to leave behind what makes you feel safe, you too can take your own giant leap.

Let's go back to the example we previously discussed. Guess what happens in the closing scene of *Good Will Hunting*? We see Will step out of his comfort zone, leaving everything behind, heading to California.

Where will you go when you leave yours?

PART 3:

PEAK PERFORMANCE

"Expect problems and eat them for breakfast."

- Alfred A. Montapert

"Do you want to know who you are? Don't ask. Act! Action will delineate and define you."

- Thomas Jefferson

"Ain't no man can avoid being born average, but there ain't no man got to be common."

- Satchel Paige

Chapter Eleven:

Commitment: Lions, Chickens, Pigs and You

If you like to have bacon and eggs for breakfast, I've got a question for you.

When it comes to bacon and eggs, what's the difference between the chicken and the pig?

Answer: The chicken is *involved*, but the pig is *committed.*

Yes, the chicken obviously lays the eggs, but the pig, unfortunately, is the bacon. You can't get much more committed than that!

Now lets tie that into business. Many of my clients are business owners. They are also totally committed to those businesses. Other clients are in senior leadership positions and their compensation is tied directly to the company's profit performance. By virtue of this "shared success" model, they are also committed to their organizations. They win when the organization wins. And when the organization loses…well, you guessed it. So do they.

That means they are the "pigs" of this metaphor. If the company has a downturn, they will find themselves in the frying pan.

Then there are the "chickens." The chickens are the employees who come to work, lay a few eggs (do their work) and go home at night. They are obviously involved, and they probably care about doing their job well, care about their co-workers, and the customers.

But it's still a job. They usually get paid the same whether the company's having a good or bad year. What they worry about the most is job security.

Obviously, workers will maintain a completely different mindset based on whether they are a chicken or a pig. There is a significant gap between the way employees (chickens) and owners and stakeholders (pigs) think. The pigs will do whatever it takes to create success—and the chickens will do whatever it takes to earn their paycheck.

What's a smart pig to do? Well, the smart pig should figure out how to turn his chickens into fellow pigs. They're much more compatible. If everyone is invested to perform at the same level, the work product will be better.

In the healthiest of organizations, there is a culture of *shared success*. If you're an owner or senior leader, you should be asking yourself:

How do employees benefit when the organization wins?

If you believe it is because they get to keep their jobs, then you will inevitably produce a workplace full of poultry. They'll get the job done, but they'll be missing the essential spark that can take a company from good to great.

To turn employees into porkers, it takes more than just financial benefits. As a matter of fact, your benefit "package" should contain such essential elements as gratitude, recognition and the potential for advancement. Something as simple and easy as a private "thank you" or even public praise promotes a shared success culture, and "owner thinking." Suddenly, you'll find your chickens are becoming increasingly pigheaded.

Now...what if you're a chicken who wants to be a pig, but management's not interested in changing your species?

Change it yourself. When you're confronted with a work challenge, ask yourself, "*What would the owner do?*" Don't limit yourself to involvement. Instead, be *committed* to the achievements of the organization.

Of course, you might be asking, "What's in it for me?" Why should you up your level of caring?

Because there is a huge pay-off if you do—if only in your own personal development. When you take the time to train yourself in "the way of the pig," you change your mindset from that of a passive employee to a take-charge leader. The more you think that way, the more you're setting yourself up for success, either within the organization you're currently working for or for another one in the future. You might even find yourself planning your *own* venture.

So don't be too chicken to encourage the development of more pigs—or even to become one yourself.

But wait—I'm going to add another animal to this chapter's menagerie. In order to become a pig, you have to find your inner lion.

I talked about that lion in Chapter 5, but I'm going to go more in-depth here. Before you can really commit to outside endeavors, you have to commit to inside endeavors. When you look in the mirror, you shouldn't just see yourself—you should see that growling overgrown cat that welcomes us to every MGM movie.

You can't control the outcomes, but you *can* control the inputs. Your commitment to yourself and your goals must be absolute.

That commitment requires two essential ingredients: *optimism* and *confidence*. You have to believe you can be successful *before you start*.

"But wait a minute," you might be saying to this chapter, "how can I know I'll be successful? There's no guarantee of that."

There's no guarantee of anything except that if you feel beaten before you start, you most assuredly will end up beaten.

Here's a little secret about how the mind works. If what you imagine is vivid enough, your subconscious can't tell the difference between it and reality. When you practice the right visualizations, you prepare your mind for success. Visualizing the desired outcome *is actually half the battle.*

Along with those visualizations, you should use daily positive affirmations to introduce positive thoughts into your mind. So write down the daily affirmations that will keep you armed with the right mental attitude.

The other side of realizing your objectives in the real world is to put a plan together—and to schedule *massive, sustained action.* Book your success plan into your calendar.

Hire or recruit someone to hold you accountable. Give them permission to hold you accountable and think about recruiting someone who also needs you to serve as an accountability partner for *them.*

Commit to yourself, and commit to your success. Find your inner "pig-lion." You'll be a whole new kind of animal—one who isn't afraid to commit and always sets out to achieve.

I am pig...hear me roar!

Chapter Twelve:

Awareness: Are You Living Life on Autopilot?

It feels awful to miss out.

We all end up skipping parties that turned out to be awesome, missing out on concerts everybody is talking about, or not catching (or recording) the must-see TV shows that the critics are raving about.

It stings a little. Everybody wants to be a part of something special. But you sigh, move on with your life and, before you know it, you've forgotten your regret because you have to concentrate on whatever it is you have to do next.

No big deal, right?

Well, I have some bad news for you. You're missing out on something much bigger than any show, concert or party.

The event you're missing out on is your life.

Here's a fun scientific fact—did you know that your subconscious mind actually controls 95 to 98% of your thinking? And now that you do know that, do you understand the implications of that?

It means that the vast majority of the time, you are "on autopilot"—going through the motions while being controlled by pre-programmed processes in your brain of which you are not even aware.

Think about it like your computer. At any given time, you may only be performing one task on it—checking your email, surfing the web, writing a paper, watching a video, or listening to music. However, the one task you are performing accounts for just a small percentage of all the things occurring on your computer. It is simultaneously scanning for viruses, searching for updates, and so forth. It's been programmed to do all these things without your knowledge, so the technical stuff doesn't distract you.

Your brain's no different. Think about a time where you were traveling home from work. You determine you need to take a different route to swing by the grocery store and grab a few things for dinner. As you approach the turn for the grocery store, you are reflecting on your day and simply miss the turn and continue to head towards your house. Why did this happen? Because your subconscious brain just told you to make all the turns you usually do every day.

While that may represent a small inconvenience regarding your travel home, the same "autopilot" can actually negatively impact much more important areas of your life. Many of us sleepwalk through each day, doing everything we need to do, but lacking any kind of *awareness* of what we might be *capable* of doing. Unless you actively work to develop an awareness of your life or to understand the control you actually have over that life, you can lapse into a wide-awake coma. You eat when you're supposed to, you sleep when you're supposed to, you work when you're supposed to and the rest of the time you just waste precious moments.

This can be an extremely harmful way to live life. So stop running for a minute, take a deep breath, and focus on what I am about to say next.

Human beings are different from every other creature on the planet. *We're special.* And what makes us unique among all the other animals on planet Earth is that we possess the capacity to evaluate our options and to make conscious, deliberate choices. We have been blessed with this awesome power.

Sadly, many of us don't use it.

Instead, *if* we don't work on achieving awareness, we rely on our reflexes and other pre-programming to which our brains default. For example, the "fight or flight response" is an instinct, an impulse. Overeating? Overspending? Thinking small? Not stepping into your greatness? These are the damaging results of programming that keeps us repeating the same behaviors, even when we continuously achieve the same horrible results.

When you think of the control this default programming has over you, how does that make you feel? Does it displease you? Irritate you? Maybe even piss you off?

If so, it's time for a change. And that change comes in the form of switching off your "autopilot."

There's only one way I know how you can turn off your "autopilot." And, I'm afraid to say, it's going to take some hard work. There are three Points you're going to have to understand thoroughly, those three Points start with the letters, **A, B** and **O**.

Point A. Point A represents where you **A**re at today: your circumstances, the results you're achieving by your actions and decisions, the "current state" of your overall life.

Point B. Point B represents where you want to **B**e: your goals, your ambitions, the results you *want* to achieve, and the "desired state" of your life.

Point O. Point O represents the **O**bstacle that's preventing you from getting from A to B. And quite often there's more than one of those obstacles. It's your job to figure out what they are and why they're so powerful.

The culmination of these points is to begin to *study and understand your obstacles.* They undoubtedly include hidden habits and beliefs programmed inside you that are holding you back. Give them names. Hell, don't stop there; give them avatars if it helps you battle them (sometimes it's good to see what you're up against). Put them on your wall and consider how they fight your best self every single day of your life. And then figure out what you can do to overcome them.

No, I'm not kidding and I'm not crazy. You want victory over self-sabotage? You'd better come armed with the right weapons.

Awareness is one such weapon. When you are aware and when you *know* why you're not getting what you want out of your life, you can actively take steps to stop the pre-programmed madness.

So snap out of it. Turn off the autopilot switch. And turn on your awareness as well as your determination.

Step into your greatness. Conscious. Aware. Purposeful. Deliberate. You'll discover that the *best possible version of you* is waiting to come out to play.

Don't miss out on that awesome reunion.

Chapter Thirteen:

Failures You Know and Love: Jobs, Edison and Lincoln

Brace yourself—we're about to talk about failure.

Is failure really bad luck? Or is it just a stepping-stone to *good* luck?

Or…is it all about omelets? Stay with me here.

I don't know how you feel about omelets, but I love them. Whether you eat them or not, I'd be willing to bet you've heard the old expression, "If you're going to make an omelet, you have to break a few eggs."

But let's take that a step further. Here's the analogy I like to use:

Failures are to success as eggs are to omelets.

In other words, you need eggs to make omelets and you need failure to recognize, understand, and achieve success. I don't think I've ever read the story of a successful person who didn't experience any kind of failure along the way, and I've read a lot of those stories.

So let me say this again—*you have to fail in order to succeed.*

Do you believe it? If you do, you have to understand why those who have the overpowering need to succeed must also have the willingness to fall flat on their face along the way.

As a matter of fact, they must be *eager* and ready to fail. Now I know few people actually invite failure into their lives, but let's discuss why failure is critical to achieving success.

Fundamentally, the farther you want to go, the *more* you have to test yourself. When I was an engineering student, I was taught to test the strength of a piece of metal by loading it until it failed. Think about that concept as it relates to our lives. How can you recognize how much you can achieve until you "load" to failure?

Many people settle for less than what they want—or set easily obtainable goals that won't rock their world—precisely because they *don't* want to be tested. They are *scared* to fail.

If you want to *Ascend*, you have to take a leap of faith. You have to go for it as hard as you can until you fail. And when you do fail, you have to bounce back. Do this, and you will identify your *present* limitations and then be able to grow beyond those limitations based on this "negative experience."

To illustrate this, let's talk about a few "failures"...

Steve Jobs, often referred to as one of the great innovators of our time, *was fired from his own company—by a guy HE first hired!*

Now, that's failure with a capital "F."

A few years later, Apple found itself floundering without Jobs' unique vision and eventually learned from its own failure and rehired Jobs. They eventually put him back in charge. And then came the iPod, the iPad, the iPhone...and, oh yeah, Jobs also brought to life the most successful independent movie studio of all time, Pixar.

Let's talk about Thomas Edison, the great inventor who brought us the light bulb. It reportedly took him roughly *one thousand tries* until he finally came up with a successful prototype. How many of us would be willing to try *anything* one thousand times? If Edison hadn't, we'd all be watching TV by candlelight.

A reporter once asked Edison how it felt to have failed one thousand times. His response: *"I didn't fail a thousand times. The light bulb was an invention with a thousand steps."*

Speaking of inventors, consider The Great Emancipator, Abraham Lincoln. I think we can all agree that Lincoln was one of our most admired American political figures.

Well, Honest Abe lost his first election. In his second election he came in eighth out of thirteen candidates. He quit his first campaign for the Senate because he knew he didn't have enough support—so he backed another candidate instead.

He did go through with his second run for the Senate, but still lost. Two years later he was elected our 16th President.

The fact remains that if you look at Lincoln's life story, he failed countless times, not only in the political arena, but in business and in his personal life.

However, these significant setbacks both tested and benefited him. Lincoln was a piece of metal that was loaded and loaded over and over again until it failed. But through all the setbacks, Lincoln grew stronger and stronger. He was growing his political skills, his orating power, his intellectual abilities and his knowledge of how the world worked.

When he finally got to the White House, he was as prepared as a man could be—which may be why he's regarded by many as our greatest President.

Zig Ziglar said, *"Failure is an event, not a person."*

Imagine what the country would have lost, or never gained, if Abraham Lincoln had not embraced his failures and persevered. Or if, with no money or resources, Steve Jobs was discouraged while trying to invent the personal computer in his garage? Or if Edison got to the nine hundredth attempt with the light bulb and said, "Screw this bulb?"

Now, imagine what you'll wind up with if you give up on what you want. Actually, you don't have to imagine it—*because you already don't have it.* And you most likely never will unless you have your own personal miracle.

Failure is one of our greatest teachers. You shouldn't fear it—you should embrace it and learn from it.

When life knocks you down, get back up. Knocked down again? Get back up again! Take in its lesson and get back in the game.

Failure is always a prime ingredient in the true recipe for success. So start cookin'.

Chapter Fourteen:

Time: The Great One Hundred and Sixty Eight

What do Bill Gates, Bill Clinton and Bill Nye the Science Guy have in common with you?

Unless your name is Bill, it's not your first name.

But even if your name *is* Bill, those three Bills, and you, and even me each have one hundred and sixty-eight.

Not one hundred and sixty-eight dollars.

Not one hundred and sixty-eight friends on Facebook.

Not even one hundred and sixty-eight bones in your body. (There are actually two hundred and eight, said the know-it-all.)

We each have one hundred and sixty-eight hours. Every week.

One hundred and sixty-eight hours makes up your weekly "time allowance," your budget that you have to "spend" to get things done and the amount of clay you have to mold into whatever you want to achieve in those seven days.

How are you spending those hours?

Time is precious. I don't really appreciate the phrase "We picked up some extra time" because there is no such thing. We don't gain time—we lose it, no matter the situation.

And yet…how much of that limited amount of time do we fritter away?

To my way of thinking, time is more precious than gold. If you had one hundred and sixty-eight bars of gold, would you consider throwing any of them away?

So treat each moment as a precious resource, one with which you would never consider parting. Spend that precious commodity wisely, because once it's lost it is irreplaceable.

Now, let's return to the beginning of the chapter, where we mentioned the three guys named Bill. Those three Bills will help demonstrate a set of amazing life accomplishments.

Let's start with Bill Clinton. Whatever your political leanings, there's no disputing the fact that, despite humble beginnings, he reached great heights, becoming the 42nd President of the United States.

The second Bill is Bill Gates, the co-founder of Microsoft. As you know, Gates created a technological empire and now spends his precious hours giving back to the world in so many important and life-changing ways.

And the final Bill, Bill Nye the Science Guy, has become internationally recognized for his continuing efforts to educate people of all ages about science and its impact on our lives.

So, I would say the "trio of Bills" has made the most of their one hundred and sixty-eight hours per week.

But how about you?

How do you go about making the most of each hour, each of your one hundred and sixty eight "bars of gold?" This is where personal leadership and self-mastery really come into play. Personal leadership begins with the recognition that you are 100% responsible for your choices and your actions, and self-mastery provides the discipline to help you make those choices really count.

No time to exercise? Nonsense. You *choose* not to exercise.

Don't read much? Again, this is *your* choice. Shut off the TV and open a book.

Are you continuing to educate yourself? Are you involved in your community at any level? How about your spiritual development? These are important areas all of us could be working on within those one hundred and sixty-eight hours.

There is so much potential. And so much time to realize it.

I realize we can't all be world-changers. But we *are* responsible for how we use our time and manage our lives. Keep in mind you have something in common with the most successful people in the world. That is, you possess the same one hundred and sixty-eight hours, the same 10,080 minutes, and the same 604,800 seconds as all of them.

Nothing differentiates the successful from the unsuccessful more than the way they spend their time.

So use that decision-making ability properly when you're dealing with your one hundred and sixty-eight hours. Choose to read an inspirational book, to practice positive daily affirmations, to set goals, to develop a plan to reach a cherished goal, to exercise, to eat nutritious meals, to practice your faith, or to help someone less fortunate. Choose to love, to laugh, and to give thanks for the blessings you have in your life.

What are you waiting for? Go ahead. Make those choices now.

If you want to grow and to develop, you have to commit yourself to making your one hundred and sixty-eight *great.*

In the words of one more famous Bill, Bill Murray—"*That's a fact, Jack!*"

Chapter Fifteen:

To Delegate or Not to Delegate?

"Hey, I need you to take care of something for me."

How comfortable are you saying those words?

How comfortable are you with delegation?

Now, some people are way too comfortable bossing others around. But most people are *not* comfortable handing out assignments to others. There are a few common reasons for that:

- They fear being seen as "lazy" or obnoxious.
- They fear that the people receiving those assignments will hate them.
- They fear that nobody can do anything as well as they can.
- They fear that once the small and meaningless tasks are accomplished, they will be left with only the huge and overwhelming ones.

In each of these abovementioned phrases, we see a common word: "fear".

When you truly *Ascend*, you must shed weight in order to rise to a higher level. Part of the weight is manifested in the duties bogging you down that could be delegated. When you continue to do everything yourself, it prevents you from achieving more important goals.

That's why you must also shed the *fear* of letting go of those duties.

Delegation is a powerful leadership tool. By definition, it is the assignment of *meaningful* tasks, either operational or managerial, to others. Contrary to popular belief, delegation is *not* just for simple, unpopular or isolated tasks assigned at the whim of the supervisor. It works best when regular and ongoing duties are assigned to ensure the entire team is clear on their individual responsibilities.

Delegation isn't just some kind of power trip to show everyone what a big shot you are. Rather, it's an essential aspect of growing and developing a business and should be approached logically and *objectively*. It also provides big benefits as you *Ascend*.

Some the most meaningful benefits to delegating tasks in an organized and concise manner include:

Enhanced Employee Capabilities and Confidence. The more you entrust an employee with responsibilities, the more valuable they feel and the more confidence they ultimately gain from the successful management of those responsibilities. In contrast, when you don't increase their responsibilities, they feel insecure about their ability to succeed. But far worse, they will rarely feel challenged, which can lead to complacency.

Improved Teamwork. When you keep everything to yourself and only assign tasks sporadically, your team will feel uninformed and left out of the loop. This kind of foggy management also leads employees to distrust one another (and you), because they each feel as if they're somehow at a disadvantage and ultimately left out.

Improved Focus. When you're trying to do everything at once, important details will invariably slip through the cracks. However, when you have an efficient delegation system in place, those with assigned duties have the proper amount of time to concentrate on their specific tasks and responsibilities to make sure they get them done. And that's a big boost to your overall efficiency.

Added Time for Leadership Activities. You know what's easy? Making sure there's enough printer paper in the supply closet. You know what's hard? Planning for your next level of business growth, facing a difficult client situation that needs to be resolved, or identifying why revenues are declining. Losing yourself in meaningless activities to avoid the big decisions is an illogical way to do business. In order to grow, in order to be successful, *you need to plan.* Somebody else can go to Staples.

By this point, it should be clear that it is imperative to delegate responsibility. But that is the easy part. The hard part is actually doing it. So, how do you delegate responsibly and effectively while realizing the benefits? The best steps to identifying and delegating authority and tasks are as follows:

Clarify Objectives and Set Performance Standards. As already noted, it's best to be as clear as possible when it comes to managing employees. When you delegate duties, make sure those involved understand what they need to achieve and the level of achievement required by you to make this work. "Why" is also an important question that frequently gets overlooked. When a worker *understands* the reasons a task has to be completed, it helps motivate them to complete it in a quality manner.

Shift Authority Along with Responsibilities. Don't give someone more responsibility than his job level should have. By the same token, don't ask someone to take care of a task that's clearly below his pay qualifications. Certainly, there are isolated exceptions to both scenarios, but, in general, delegation works best when it's done with levels of authority in mind.

Provide Necessary Support Systems. If you ask someone to assume a new duty, it's *your* responsibility to ensure he has access to the resources needed to do the job at a high level. Otherwise, you're setting him up for failure. It's hiring a chauffeur when you don't have a car.

Establish Reasonable Checkpoints and Deadlines. This step is especially important when you've just delegated a new task. The individual to whom you delegated it may have no idea of what a reasonable timeframe for getting it accomplished should be. Or when he should check in with you along the way. Checkpoints and deadlines help avoid this problem and keep everyone on the same page.

Review Results, Not Methods. Nobody will do something exactly the same way you would do it. It's important to allow people to accomplish tasks in the manner with which they're most comfortable—unless you're not seeing the desired results. In that case, make adjustments and offer support to reach your goals.

Every delegation situation is different – but here's a seven-step process that will help you to accomplish your goals:

1. Tell them what to do.

2. Show them what to do.

3. Let them try while you observe.

4. Praise progress.

5. Repeat until competent.

6. Transfer responsibility.

7. Monitor periodically.

Again, *don't do it all yourself.* As a leader, remember that your team will support you and help you achieve your goals. But that doesn't mean all responsibilities should be delegated. Rest assured there is still plenty for you to do. These accountabilities include providing overall business leadership, developing strategy and vision, building solid channels of communication and maintaining strong relationships with *key stakeholders* (partners, vendors and customers).

Finally, you should always understand that delegation is a process and not an event. When effectively implemented, delegation can pay huge dividends to the leader, the team and the business. But it takes time and patience. As you create more structure and delegate larger roles to your team, you will find they will rise to the occasion and meet your expectations.

So take care of something for me, and don't be afraid to delegate!

Chapter Sixteen:

Listen Up!

Imagine that you are having a conversation with a friend who says…

"I just saw Bruce Springsteen perform and I can honestly say *it was the best concert I have ever seen.*"

Now, what's your *first reaction* regarding that comment?

Was it about whether or not you had ever seen Bruce Springsteen?

Or, was it about which concert you would say is the best you've ever seen?

In other words…was it all about you?

If so, welcome to the human race!

As Dr. Stephen Covey put it, we transplant our lives into other people's stories. This is what people typically do—and there's nothing abnormal about it. We try to relate and to connect.

But, what would you typically *say* to a friend who made such a statement about Bruce Springsteen?

Again, if you were like most people, you'd probably talk about whether *you've* seen The Boss in concert—or even make a reference to the best concert that *you've* seen. Because the average person quickly inserts himself into the other person's story.

And while we've established that this is a typical response, it isn't always the *best* response. At least not if you're somebody who wants to *Ascend.*

What's so bad about sharing your own experiences with The Boss?

Well, think about it from your friend's perspective. Do you believe that that friend has more to share about the experience? Of course he does. As you probably know, we enjoy reliving some of the pleasure of an event by sharing vivid descriptions of it.

With that in mind, don't deny your friend this pleasure. There will likely be a time for you (the listener) to share a similar experience, but it's too soon to immediately turn the conversation around to yourself. We can be better. *You* can be better.

We can *listen* better. That's what this chapter is all about.

The first step in learning to listen better is to be aware of what "level" we're listening at. In my experience, there are at least three levels of listening:

Level 1 Listening, also called *Internal Listening,* is the official term for the level of listening of which I just spoke. A Level 1 Listener focuses not on the speaker, but on himself. In Level 1 Listening, we take whatever we hear and make it about *us* instead of the speaker.

This is not listening at its best. For example, let's take Alice and George, a typical married couple. Alice asks George to pick up a bowl of Cheerios at the store. As a Level 1 listener, George's thoughts would immediately turn to himself. Maybe he'd suddenly experience a craving for Cheerios, wander into the kitchen and pour himself a bowl, and then wonder why Alice is suddenly giving him the death look.

Level 2 Listening is all about *Understanding.* The focus of a Level 2 Listener is geared towards the speaker. We listen to the speaker's words, tone, the volume and the pace of his speech. We also look at his expressions and body language for additional information that will help us understand the message. The downside? A Level 2 Listener is not interpreting the message or trying to "get under the hood."

Let's get back to Alice and George. If Alice makes her same request and George is listening at Level 2, George will then go to the store and look for a bowl of Cheerios, not a box.. Remember, she only asked for a bowl.

Imagine the reaction when he comes home. Probably something in the vicinity of complete and utter shock.

Level 3 Listening, or *Global Listening,* is widely considered the highest quality of listening. It takes time and practice to master. Global Listening is speaker focused, but goes deeper than that of Level 2. Beneath the words of the speaker are contextual clues about the speaker's message. The Level 3 Listener immerses himself in the presence of the speaker, tapping into his intuition, picking up on the emotion and intent of the overall message. What is the speaker's energy level? How does the speaker feel? The emphasis is not just about what is said, but also the hidden clues and underlying meaning.

So, if Alice asks for that bowl of Cheerios and George is practicing as a Level 3 Listener, he will realize she probably wants an entire *box* of cereal, even though she only asked for a bowl. Based on Alice's statement, George may quickly determine she is stressed and tired, and cater to her hidden clues by inquiring if she needs anything else *besides* Cheerios.

Like maybe a break, or massage or even a vacation.

See what you can learn when you really *listen*?

Pioneering psychiatrist Karl Menninger said, *"Listening is a magnetic and strange thing, a creative force. The friends who listen to us are the ones we move toward. When we are listened to, it creates us, makes us unfold and expand."*

In other words, when you listen to people effectively, they will ultimately feel valued and important. Plus, you get better information, which will help *you* on your path to being a better person.

So what steps can you take to make sure your listening reverberates at Level 3, and is not stuck at Level 1? The most effective listeners:

- Focus on the person speaking
- Try to understand instead of judge
- Imagine the experience being described
- Are not seeking to protect themselves or be defensive

Since this may not come naturally to everyone, together, let's consider the crucial steps you can take to become an effective listener.

THE 7 KEYS TO EFFECTIVE LISTENING

Key 1: Attending: This includes providing non-verbal cues that demonstrate you are aware of the person speaking. These include nodding, direct eye contact and an open and accepting posture.

Key 2: Paraphrasing: Briefly restating the basic message. By doing this, you demonstrate to the speaker that you are actively listening to the overall message.

Key 3: Reflecting: Acknowledging the feelings that you've heard or perceived. This requires you to go deeper and begin to assimilate the message into your own life.

Key 4: Probing: Asking for clarification or more information in a positive way. This will challenge your speaker to offer more information than he or she initially intended to give to you.

Key 5: Verifying: Checking that your perceptions or interpretations are accurate. By doing so, you will confirm that your understanding of the intended message is accurate.

Key 6: Being Quiet: Giving the speaker time to pause, think and continue. However, remember to be an active listener or your speaker may think you checked out of the conversation.

Key 7: Summarizing: Bringing together the experience and feelings expressed. Note that you don't have to agree, just to prove to the speaker that you listened and "got it."

By practicing those seven keys you'll become a much more effective listener. Author Bryant McGill said, *"One of the most sincere forms of respect is actually listening to what another has to say."* Listening does more than just maximize communication. It builds relationships, shows respect and allows you to learn and connect on a higher level. It takes patience, time and a sincerity we have to work at to develop. Most of us just don't come hard-wired with those traits. But through practice and diligence, you too can listen at an enormously high level.

Chapter Seventeen:

Master Your Mindset: Building a Bigger Tank

In one of my favorite group exercises, the leader asks a roomful of participants to stand up and reach up as high as they can.

So they reach.

Then, after a few seconds, the leader asks everyone to reach just a little higher.

And they actually *reach higher.*

Talk about ascending!

But wait…how could this happen? Did these people all defy the laws of physics? How could they possibly reach *"a little higher"* when they were supposedly reaching *as high as they could?*

The answer is that they were actually holding back the first time. Maybe they didn't realize it. Maybe they didn't hold back *consciously.* But there was certainly some reserve in the tank.

And accessing that reserve is a matter of mindset.

In order to *Ascend*, it is imperative for you to develop the mindset to reach beyond your current state and access that little extra. This enables you to push yourself beyond *"as high as you can"* and go just *"a little higher."*

Not just once, but all the time and all the way. Consistently, every day and in everything you try.

When it comes to reaching a little higher, *your* tank is not like your gas tank. In just about every area of your life, I promise you there are reserves you don't even know you have.

For example, maybe you have an important goal that you want to achieve. You feel like you're too busy, too stressed, or too overwhelmed to get there. Yet you still somehow find the time to watch television.

There—right there—is the reserve in your tank. So if most of us leave reserve in the tank, *what do the best do*? They empty the tank on every occasion. And then they build a bigger tank and empty that one as well. In other words, they incrementally improve. It doesn't happen all at once, they do it in stages.

They get 10% better on a daily or weekly basis.

Imagine two people. Person A is earning $100 per month. Person B is earning a constant $5,000 per month. Clearly, Person B is more successful, right?

Not if Person A accesses her reserves.

Let's say Person A increases her earning by 10% every month. After five years, Person B will still be earning $5,000 per month. While in the last month of that fifth year, Person A will earn $27,680.

My point is that the power of incremental performance is amazingly effective.

Think about sports. What is the difference between an 88 mph fastball and a 97 mph heater? Most analysts will tell you those measly 9 miles per hour separate a minor league pitcher from a Hall of Famer.

Be a little better today than you were yesterday—a little smarter, a little nicer, a little more caring, even a little more hardworking—and it will pay amazing dividends down the road.

Sometimes we don't reach higher because our mindset won't let us. If you're feeling stressed out, you might not care if there's any reserve in your tank.

So, how do we maintain a positive attitude during stressful times? How do we fight off that stinkin' thinkin' that draws us back to the couch and keeps us from reaching even higher?

Here's how I do it.

I am not a gambler. When I go to Las Vegas I don't get near the tables. Nevertheless, my favorite metaphor for a positive attitude is called House Money.

Imagine you are going to Las Vegas for a three-day conference and that you have saved $10,000.00 with which to gamble. You're not an experienced gambler, so you're fairly excited and more than a bit nervous. You go out the first evening with your gambling money and you do extremely well, winning enough to amass a bankroll of $40,000.00. You decide to deposit $30,000.00 into your bank account back home—that's your original $10,000.00, plus $20,000.00 of your winnings.

The remaining $10,000.00 can be considered House Money. You didn't have this money when you arrived in Las Vegas. If you lose it, you'll still arrive home with a bigger bank account than when you left.

You still have two days to gamble for fun. With this safety net in place, how would you feel and behave during the rest of your time in Las Vegas?

When I discuss this with clients and friends, the overwhelming answer is that they would feel little stress or worry and feel pretty positive.

Now, what if I told you that you could adopt this mindset at any time?

Try it. Play a trick on yourself the next time you're feeling a stressful situation manifest itself in your life. Ask, "How would I act and feel if I knew that this could not harm me?"

And then, do it! Pretend it's true and act accordingly. Suspend your disbelief and behave as if there was no stress, no worry, no negativity.

Interviewing for a job you really need? Pretend that you don't need the job but want it because the job is really interesting to you.

Dreading a difficult conversation with a friend, co-worker, boss or anyone else? Imagine that you know the conversation will be successful because you maintained your composure and your focus on being positive.

The key is to "suspend your disbelief" and unleash the power of positive thinking.

How high would you reach if you knew nothing could stop you?

Do it. Then reach a little higher.

Chapter Eighteen:

Results Matter – or, Why ROV Beats KLT

In the business world, rapport building is all the rage. "People Buy People" is the mantra of the day, and charisma and wit are now said to be the one-two punch in the battle for the hearts and minds (and dollars) of the people we meet.

It *is* far better to have charisma and excellent communication skills than to attempt relationship building without them.

But beyond that, I still find myself wondering, "Is that all there is?"

In several recent books and even a few webinars on selling, the emphasis on KLT has been enormous. KLT is an acronym for Know, Like, Trust—and the principle is as follows:

All things being equal, people would rather do business with people that they Know, Like and Trust.

It sounds simple enough. And to be honest, I find the principle to be true, despite the fact that all things are never really equal. My problem is that the principle should add *three more letters* to the end: the letters TFT, which stand for "The First Time." Because after that first time someone buys from you, hires you or adds you to a project team, the KLT factor gives way to what I call the ROV factor.

ROV stands for Results, Outcomes, and Value.

You may get a job or an assignment because someone knows you, likes you and trusts you. It happens all of the time in each and every sector of business. But if you want to *keep* the job, *retain* the customer and *win referrals* from that customer, you had better focus on producing results. Because in the end, you have to deliver.

In other words, what do you actually add to the equation? What value to do you bring to the enterprise? How do you help the employer/team/ client in terms of time, money and work product? You'd better be able to produce more in value than in cost, or you will be cast aside—regardless of how charismatic and witty you are.

Before you spend too much time trying to be known, liked and trusted, I suggest that you concentrate on creating value that your customers, clients or employers desire and of which they can't get enough.

Do this, and the KLT will take care of itself.

The goal should be to be known, liked and trusted for producing serious *results.*

So, how can you make sure your KLT continues to translate into ROV?

Well, here's another question for you. How much weight can you lift?

How could you determine *precisely* how much weight you are able to lift?

There are only two ways that I know of to accurately answer this question. The first is to start with a relatively light weight and then add to it until you can no longer lift it. The second is to start with a weight that is very heavy and then remove weight until you can lift it.

Either way, you will find your limit through *experimentation.*

In my experience, that is also true of most aspects of our lives. You don't know your limits until you reach them. It's only when we reach those limits that we learn about ourselves, that we challenge ourselves and that we are really able to experience growth.

Reflect back on the times in your life when things were easy and effortless. Or when your KLT attracted lots of new customers, clients or projects.

Be careful. Because those are the times when we are susceptible to complacency. Even to stagnation.

Now, I've got nothing against good times and the great feeling you get when a plan comes together. It's simply that we should be real about *where* and *when* growth occurs.

If you were forced to choose between living *inside* your comfort zone, living *outside* of it, or living on *the edge*...where would you live? It's a personal question, with no absolute right or wrong answer.

But for my money, build me a house right on the edge. In fact, just a little over the edge.

We all know challenging times facilitate growth. But the real question is: how do we make sure we keep experiencing challenges so we continue our growth?

How do we fight the complacency that creeps in precisely *because* things are going well?

We can just allow life to unfold, remaining receptive to challenges and welcoming them as an opportunity for growth. In fact, this is a healthy attitude.

Or, we can actively seek out opportunities to get out of our comfort zone.

One Memorial Day weekend, I had one such opportunity with my sons, David and Brian. We participated in a friend's adrenaline-filled retreat in the hills of Tennessee. Now I've been on retreats, and I have to be honest—this wasn't really what I'd call a retreat. It was the opposite of a retreat. It was more like an attack weekend! We went fast on the ground, we went fast in the water and we went fast in the air climbing trees, jumping off trees and generally scaring ourselves silly over and over again.

Even better though, we spent just as much time reflecting on some of life's most important questions. The amazing thing I discovered is: your answers change when your pulse hits 140 BPM and you find yourself shooting paintballs out of the helicopter with no doors (no joke).

While I don't know if your answers would be different, I do know that mine were. They were more real, less filtered, authentic and genuine, and way more helpful. And that was the point.

Get yourself out of your comfort zone, then quickly look back on your life and assess it. *Who are you? What are you here for? What is most important to you? What do you claim to be your values?*

Now, is the way that you conduct yourself consistent with your answers to those questions?

If you are not "walking your talk," you have three choices:

1) Change your walk

2) Change your talk, or

3) Remain a hypocrite. Does that sting? Yep, it stung me too. Follow that sting to the source. Then eliminate it.

And not only will you develop an enviable KLT quotient, you'll also deliver the kind of ROV that will keep people coming back for more.

Results. Outcomes. Value.

Chapter Nineteen:

Conquer Your Competition – with a Little Help from a 2500-Year-Old Book

Consider the book *The Art of War.*

Penned approximately 2500 years ago by a Chinese general named Sun Tzu, this book is often cited not only by famous generals like Colin Powell, but also political leaders, business gurus and big shots from other walks of life. In fact, today there are special, modern editions of the book designed exclusively for executives and managers.

Now, you might be wondering what some 2500-year-old Chinese guy could possibly know about doing business in the modern age of smart phones and iPads. Let alone regular warfare in the age of predator drones.

I don't think they even had guns in Ancient China.

But what makes Sun Tzu's book incredibly relevant after thousands of years of technological and societal change is one irrevocable fact.

Things change. But *people* don't.

2500 years later—and a half a world away from Sun Tzu's stomping ground—human nature remains essentially the same.

And at its core, *The Art of War* is a book about understanding and triumphing over human nature. Or, as the book surmises, conflict may be an inevitable part of life, but we all possess the tools to deal with and triumph over it.

As a success coach, I completely agree with Sun Tzu. Not only do I believe conflict is inevitable, I welcome those inevitable conflicts as they offer incredible opportunities for personal and professional growth. So I fully recommend reading and understanding *The Art of War.*

Because if you don't, chances are your competition already has.

To give you a head start, I'm going to share with you my own brief, abbreviated take on some of the most relevant parts of *The Art of War:*

Preparation: *"Battles are won or lost before they are fought."*

The difference between winning and losing a battle may be as simple as preparation. Victorious warriors win first and *then* go to war, while defeated warriors first go to war and then seek the win.

This teaching emphasizes the importance of planning and preparation to effective execution. Practice doesn't make perfect. Perfect practice makes perfect. In other words, if you want to win, don't add a "g" to that word and "*wing it.*"

Study: *"Keep your friends close, but your enemies closer."*

This teaching refers to studying your competition, learning what makes them tick, what they're all about, and comparing what they have to what you have. Competitive analysis may seem to be a lost practice. But today, smart businesses continue to study their competition closely. Whoever your adversaries may be in life, don't shut them out. Keep them close and learn from them.

Deception: *"All warfare is based upon deception."*

National Football League great Barry Sanders said that he had only two moves: "fake right and go left" and "fake left and go right." His repertoire may have been limited, but he was so deceptive with those two moves that he was extremely effective on the field. So much so that he is considered one of the greatest running backs in the history of the NFL.

The art of deception isn't about lying, cheating, and being a person of poor character. In the business world, it's simply about outmaneuvering your competition. These maneuvers can take many forms, from providing better service to customers, to being more responsive to market needs, to treating your people better, to out-thinking your competitors. Which isn't exactly deceptive. It's just smart.

Leadership: *"A leader leads by example, not by force."*

If you don't "walk your talk," it's hard to expect others to follow. Of course, there are leaders out there who use force to compel action from their teams. However, such "leaders" are not successful, at least not in the long run.

The best leaders give their teams something to which they can aspire, creating a culture of success and accountability that flows from the top down.

Process and Communication: *"To control many is the same as controlling few, using formations and signals."*

"Formations and signals" sounds like battle, right? Well, change the terms to processes and communication and voila, you've got the same principle applied to the business world.

The most successful organizations use easily duplicated processes and effective communication to consistently reach their objectives. When everyone is on the same page, it makes for a powerful read.

Commanders: *"Demonstrate wisdom, sincerity, humanity, courage and firmness."*

People buy into the leader before they buy into his vision. How many of these positive qualities above do you demonstrate? Also, consider the opposite of these characteristics—stupidity, artificiality, coldness, cowardice and being wishy-washy. Don't be those. People hate them and they'll hate you. Nothing personal.

I hope that you find my synopsis of *The Art of War* helpful and enticing enough to propel you to purchase this amazing and time-relevant book. I promise, it will be an investment that pays dividends for you, your career and your business.

Also, it's the only 2500-year-old Chinese book that I really urge people to read.

Chapter Twenty:

Resourcefulness – or, Calling on Your Inner MacGyver

If you were around in the '80s, you may remember a popular television show called *MacGyver.* The show's lead character was a secret agent named Angus MacGyver—and his claim to fame (besides sporting one of the greatest mullets in television history) was his amazing ability to develop incredible solutions to seemingly unsolvable problems.

Using only his intelligence, ingenuity and whatever happened to be around (usually duct tape was somehow involved), MacGyver built complex devices from the simplest of components. Some of his best include:

- Fixing a blown fuse with a gum wrapper
- Turning an ordinary basement pipe into a wall-destroying torpedo
- Using water and a raw egg to repair a tear in a car radiator
- Combining a stethoscope, a blood pressure cuff and an alarm clock to make a homemade lie detector

Okay, maybe the show was a bit unrealistic. But I loved it anyway.

Looking back, the reason the show resonated so strongly with me wasn't because of the suspense or the drama or the action scenes. I loved *MacGyver* because, at his core, Angus MacGyver was all about *resourcefulness.*

Which is a quality that can come in pretty handy while you're attempting to *Ascend.*

A book about ascending wouldn't really be complete without mentioning resourcefulness. Why? Well, if you follow the advice in this book, you will push yourself and likely find yourself in some challenging situations.

When it becomes apparent that you're in one of those situations, you may feel at a loss. You may wonder what to do when what you've always done just won't work.

But what would MacGyver do? He would be resourceful.

That's why this concept is so important. Just like MacGyver, you have the ability to triumph over even the most baffling and difficult scenarios.

Like our fictional hero, you also possess a largely untapped body of resourcefulness.

How do I know? I see it all the time. It's part of my job. One of the benefits of my job coaching leaders to achieve even higher levels of greatness is when I get an opportunity to witness a client getting in touch with a previously unknown capability.

In other words, when that client taps into his or her inner resourcefulness. This is a process where the capability actually *emerges from within.* Where you discover that you had it in you the whole time.

But I am willing to bet you're considering from where your resourcefulness can arise.

Resourcefulness is simply a matter of suspending your disbelief about a limitation you *thought* you had, or a challenge you *thought* there was no way you could overcome. When you let that disbelief go and concentrate your energy on finding a solution, that's when incredible things happen.

You may never be able to repair a blown fuse with a gum wrapper, but you will discover that you have capabilities far greater than those that you regularly utilize.

Trust me. I'm off to build an airplane with an old Volkswagen, a washing machine, a hotplate and some duct tape.

Always gotta have the duct tape.

PART 4:
ASCENDING TO THE NEXT LEVEL

"The greater danger for most of us lies not in setting our aim too high and falling short; but in setting our aim too low, and achieving our mark."

- Michelangelo

"I have tried to keep on with my striving because this is the only hope I have of ever achieving anything worthwhile and lasting."

- Arthur Ashe

"Students achieving Oneness will move on to Twoness."

- Woody Allen

Chapter Twenty One:

Welcome the Critic

Does it ever feel like all you hear is the sound of one hand clapping when you accomplish something?

Or worse, maybe you hear someone say, "Well, that was okay, but if you had done it a different way, you'd probably get an even better result."

You're not alone. As the saying goes, "Everybody's a critic." And it feels like those amateur critics are always reviewing *you*.

Unfortunately, that is the nature of society. Friends, family, business associates—heck, even the checkout guy at the supermarket could be thinking your sweater is ugly, right?

Maybe this is why all those daytime TV court shows are so popular. It's just fun to see some *other* poor souls judged for a couple of minutes.

People constantly size up one another. We are always comparing ourselves to colleagues, friends, even people we barely know. Of course, judgment can also be an act of aggression. When we feel someone threatens our position we will often think, or even express, negative opinions to build ourselves up at the other person's expense.

Whatever the reason, judgment is always around us. We're surrounded by it. Like James Bond trying to outrun a squadron of assassins, we find that *the critics just keep coming.*

But unlike James Bond, we have no chance of stopping them.

So, what should our response be?

Welcome the critic.

This is a relatively new development in my consciousness. For many years, I definitely did *not* welcome the critic. I wanted the critic captured and imprisoned with no shot at release.

As far as I was concerned, critics brought people down. They stopped them from achieving. Critics cut apart confidence and chopped self-esteem into pieces. I used to believe a critic's goal was to build himself up and tear others down, causing a lot of unnecessary emotional pain for those on the receiving end.

But then I learned about the concept of *constructive* criticism. And I learned it from a magnificent teacher.

That instructor was my former boss. He assisted me in "earning and learning" my way into a challenging leadership position. When I performed well, he let me know it and reinforced that success.

However, he also took advantage of opportunities to be critical of my efforts. In other words, when I screwed up, he let me know how and why. Most importantly, in a non-threatening way, he helped me understand what I did wrong.

Through this relationship, I learned *constructive criticism can be remarkably helpful.* But only if you're willing to listen to it.

And that can be a big "if." Columnist Franklin Jones said, "*Honest criticism is hard to take, particularly from a relative, friend, acquaintance or a stranger.*"

Nevertheless, I learned how to deal with it. And I took away from the experience two very powerful lessons in how to deliver constructive criticism.

Lesson #1: Praise in public and criticize in private.

There's no reason to pick someone apart in front of everyone else, unless you're on a power trip. But there's every reason to give someone a little love in front of a group—it's a positive act that makes everybody feel good. If and when you do need to criticize behavior, do so in a positive manner and behind closed doors. It will inevitably keep morale high and pushback low.

Lesson #2: Criticize actions and results, if you must, but **never criticize the person** who took the actions.

In other words, as they say in church, separate the "sin" from the "sinner." If someone forgets to do something, it really doesn't help the situation when you call him or her "stupid." That's just your anger talking. On the other hand, it's a totally different vibe when you take the approach of, "I know you have a lot on your plate, but you forgot to take care of..." In that capacity, you show understanding and empathy and still get your point across.

So how do you go about creating the proper attitude to both accept and receive criticism?

First of all, don't be afraid to have an open mind. When criticism comes their way, most people's first instinct is to be defensive. They'll either attack the critic to deflect attention, or instantly produce a laundry list of excuses to minimize the situation.

In other words, they don't actually *listen* to the noise. They're much more interested in turning it down. And they may miss an opportunity to soak in some valid feedback that could improve them significantly.

When you receive criticism, a meaningful way to lower your guard and review it objectively is to simply *externalize* it.

By that I mean you should imagine that the criticism is *not* being directed at you, but at someone that happens to have the same name as you. Did this "other person" really screw up? Could he or she have done things better? Think it through. When you externalize criticism, you escape the trap defensiveness sets and can be open to the possibility that the person saying these things *is trying to help you.*

In many cases, criticism is a good thing. As a matter of fact, if you're not getting *any* criticism, that could very well be a *bad* thing. Welcome the critic. If you're not sure the criticism is valid, ask those involved in the situation for their honest opinion. If you do think the criticism is valid, take it to heart and look for ways to improve your performance. Constructive criticism is a primary key to growth. If we don't know (or aren't willing to admit to) what we're doing wrong, how will we ever learn to do it right?

Yes, you may feel like you're in an Adam Sandler movie and the world is *The New York Times* film critic. But with an open, objective mind and a lot of work, you just might make yourself into an Oscar winner.

Chapter Twenty Two:

Character: The Best Reputation Management System

Maybe I'm just getting old.

(Mea Culpa: that's not a maybe, I <u>am</u> getting old.)

But I really do believe sometimes that the world has gone bonkers.

Mind you, I do recognize the value and welcome diversity of opinion. It would truly be a boring world if we all agreed about everything.

Thus, I would like to take exception to a new trend I'm seeing more and more of these days. That is: *Reputation Management.*

I constantly see and hear advertisements on the web and through the airwaves from companies willing to help me manage my reputation.

Thanks, but no thanks.

Reputation is made up of what other people think about you. That's not a concept with which I have a quarrel. No doubt reputation is important both in business and our personal lives. I think of it as everyone's "advance man"—moving ahead of each of us into the world to let people who may have never met us know what we're all about.

Of course, there is one very big difference. That is, you can control what your advance man says about you. When it comes to your reputation, it's in the hands of other people. So you can't control what they say, what they think or what they do. You can only *influence* their view of you, but you can't *tell* them what that view should be.

And even if you did, it tends to backfire. Your reputation becomes that of "the weirdo who tells me why I need to think he's great."

So, when it comes to reputation management, what can you actually "manage?"

The answer is that you have total control over **your character**.

Abraham Lincoln said, *"Character is like a tree and reputation like a shadow. The shadow is what we make of it; the tree is the real thing."*

So how's your tree growing? Is it gnarly, dark and twisted? Or is it strong, tall and beautiful with branches spreading out confidently into the world?

Your "tree"—your character—is *what is actually true about you.* No matter how much you try to fake it, your character (good or bad) will always shine through.

Some of us may deny this, but character can be managed. Character can be controlled. **Character can be built.** I'll go one step further. The most important ingredient in a great businessperson, a great leader, a great parent, a great *anything* **is not** intellect, charisma, vision, attitude or talent. Although these are all important, *the most important ingredient is character.*

Who you are determines what you become.

So what exactly makes up your character? Many things. A few key aspects are honesty, integrity, gratitude, discipline, respect, responsibility and compassion. *When you plan and execute around these values on a daily basis, you will automatically build a strong character.*

Here are a few ideas to help strengthen yours:

- Improve your mind by reading something useful.
- Do something good for someone with no need for affirmation. Be grateful and give thanks where deserved. Be respectful of all people, especially those with whom you disagree.
- Be compassionate and show it—share your time, your talent and your treasure.
- Take responsibility for your actions and your results. Don't play the blame game.
- Don't find fault in others. Use opportunities to improve yourself. Make promises and commitments. Then keep them.

Take these steps every day and you won't need to worry about your reputation, let alone "manage" it.

Of course, you might say, "Well, sometimes people say bad things about others that aren't true. Sometimes it doesn't matter how strong you make your character if someone is out to tarnish your reputation."

When that happens, the truth eventually wins out, especially if you're consistent in displaying positive values. People believe what they see more than what they hear. Enough people will vouch for you and nip those lies in the bud.

Who needs to "manage" their reputations?

- Hollywood stars who repeatedly get arrested.
- Politicians who cut sleazy deals and betray their constituency.

- Business people who have no respect for those they work for, work with and supervise.

- Professional athletes caught doping.

People *without* character need to manage their reputations.

Make sure you don't.

Chapter Twenty Three:

"But...That's Not What I Meant!"

"The single biggest problem in communication is the illusion that it has taken place."

Pretty clever, huh? Well, George Bernard Shaw was a pretty smart guy. Now, I never met the man, but let me make some assumptions about what he meant by this statement, and let me put it in my own inimitable words:

The intended message is rarely the same as the message that is received.

Most of us recognize this concept from playing a simple childhood game called "Telephone." For those unfamiliar with this game, it starts with one person whispering a sentence into another person's ear. That person then whispers it to the next person, and so on and so forth. When the last person in the game gets the sentence whispered in their ear, he or she then repeats the phrase.

It rarely has anything to do with the original sentence.

Why? Because one person mishears a word and another mishears another word, until the errors pile up and the original meaning is completely lost.

These same communication flaws happen in our everyday adult lives for countless reasons including issues language, gender, age, feelings, tonality, volume, accents, slang, misinterpreted humor, etc... Subtle differences and nuances of language can be the difference between communicating effectively and ineffectively.

Even some of our greatest leaders—who were considered amazing communicators in their time—have sometimes missed the mark. John F. Kennedy's famous 1963 line *"Ich bin ein Berliner,"* for example, has two meanings:

"I am one with the people of Berlin," or,

"I am a jelly donut."

Luckily, the people of Berlin chose to interpret it as the former and not the latter, and thus did not attempt to dunk our 35th President into a giant cup of coffee.

Obviously, the *context* of his remarks allowed the Germans to recognize the intended meaning. That was a no-brainer. But many messages are not. Beyond the context, we can distort meaning through our subjective "screening system." Our own beliefs and values can easily prejudice what we hear, while voids in our experience and knowledge can cause us to not really understand the overall message, even though we may *think* we completely get it.

That's an important concept to keep top of mind when you are communicating something that's important. Resist the natural assumption that the message you're sending is the message they're hearing, and then focus on being *clear.*

Of course, some think they can get around this kind of ambiguity through other means, such as writing the message down in plain black and white. Sure. Nobody ever misunderstood an email.

For example, here's how easy it can be to create confusion with just a simple statement. Consider the following sentence: *"I never said that you stole my bicycle."*

Just eight words. Eight simple words.

But try this. Say that sentence out loud six times, each time *emphasizing* a different one of these words *("I," "said," "you," "stole," "my," "bicycle")*.

A different emphasis throws a pretty good change-up, don't you think? So what do you think the original sentence was supposed to mean? What's the correct and accurate interpretation? What was the intended message?

That's hard to say. And that's the point.

Clear communication is critical. And can sometimes be extremely difficult.

A great way to improve your own personal communication skills is to be conscious of how people might misinterpret what you're saying (or writing). Mentally review your messages to make sure you didn't leave room for error.

Even better, ask the person with whom you're communicating to *confirm his understanding.* If necessary, ask him to repeat back to you the gist of your statements. This is probably the best way to confirm the two of you are communicating effectively.

It's just like how airplane pilots and air traffic controllers communicate with one another: They confirm their understanding of messages by repeating back what the other just said. And they also use active listening such as "Roger that," "Tango, bravo, whiskey, niner," in order to ensure clear communication.

Well, okay, it's not *always* clear. Conversations like this can easily happen:

Unknown Aircraft:	*"Hello?"*
Control Tower:	*"Please say again."*
Unknown Aircraft:	*"What?"*
Control Tower:	*"Who is this?"*
Unknown Aircraft:	*"This is Joe"*
Control Tower:	*"This is the control tower, where are you?"*

Unknown Aircraft: *"I'm in the plane!"*

Control Tower: *"Joe, where is the pilot?"*

Unknown Aircraft: *"He got out when the engine quit."*

Control Tower: *"Joe, what does your airspeed indicator read?"*

Unknown Aircraft: *(long pause) "Zero?"*

Control Tower: *"Joe, whatever you have in front of you—a stick or a steering wheel—push it forward. You need to get airspeed over your wings!"*

Unknown Aircraft: *"Are you sure?"*

Control Tower: *"Yes Joe! You need to push it forward! (pause) What does your airspeed indicator read now?"*

Unknown Aircraft: *"Uh, it's still zero."*

Control Tower: *(frantically scanning the sky for a falling aircraft) "Joe, where is your plane?"*

Unknown Aircraft: *"We are parked down at the end of the runway. The pilot got out when the engine quit and walked back to the hanger."*

Control Tower: *"Joe, get off the radio."*

If the above exchange seems clear to you, you've probably misunderstood what I've said in this chapter.

Roger, over and out.

Chapter Twenty Four:

Leader, Lead Thyself

As you *Ascend*, it would be only natural to discover that more and more people are looking up to you with great respect and admiration. After all, you are in lift-off mode. When people look up to you, they tend to regard you as a *leader*, leading us to consider an interesting question: Out of all the people who you might lead in your life, which one is the most important?

The most important person you lead is the *first* person that you lead.

And no, I'm not talking about your first employee, or the oldest child or player on a team that you coach.

I'm talking about *you*.

If you ever intend to be an effective leader, you must first master the art and science of leading *yourself.* As President Harry Truman said, "*In reading the lives of great men, I found that the first victory they won was over themselves...self-discipline with all of them came first.*"

Mastering self-leadership or self-discipline is the key to success. Without it, you are unlikely to achieve anything worthwhile or lasting. Luckily, self-leadership is a habit that can be formed.

In order to acquire self-leadership, you should have a strong sense of purpose, or a clear picture of where you are headed. Here's a quick exercise to help you pin that down:

Imagine that you have been granted three wishes. What would you wish for?

Now, out of those three wishes, which is most important?

That wish may not precisely pinpoint your purpose in life, but it certainly provides a clue.

Now, back to self-leadership. Those who have yet to develop the habit of self-discipline avoid tasks because they focus on the effort required. In their minds, effort is connected to *pain*. However, you can easily alter this association. When facing a new task, focus instead on the *pleasure* you will experience when you accomplish it rather than the pain you could potentially feel.

Follow these basic steps to build self-discipline and begin your ascent:

1. **Acknowledge that you are responsible.** Think of the term as "response able."

2. **Welcome internal resistance.** You need it so that you can overcome it.

3. **Visualize success**. Relax. Release any tension.

4. **Eliminate distractions.** Focus on the task at hand and the desired outcome.

5. **Take action**. Immediate action. Massive action.

6. **Relish your accomplishment.** Acknowledge that you won the battle against sloth, procrastination, and laziness.

Repeat this behavior again while attempting to achieve your next goal and savor your new ability to keep yourself under control. Acknowledge how proud you are of your actions. As you repeatedly apply these steps, your inspiration and motivation will carry you through until a habit is finally formed.

Once you have mastered the practice of self-leadership, you can truly begin to lead others. That's one of the interesting things about leadership. Real leadership comes from *inside* and is projected outward.

It doesn't come from wearing the most expensive suit, or driving the fastest car, or moving to the corner office, or obtaining the most intimidating title, or by gaining any position of authority inside an organization.

Of course, these are all accomplishments we associate with leadership. But as impressive as these credentials may appear to be, they aren't indicators of *actual* leadership—they're only the trappings of power. Plenty of leaders possess these trappings, but trappings alone don't make leaders.

The reason why is *power* and *leadership* are actually two very different animals.

Power is all about strength. It's about the capacity to control others or to force things to happen. It's about *making* people do things, but leaving them feeling like they did not want to do them in the first place.

On the other hand, leadership is a measure of your ability to *influence* others. Not to order them, not to force them, but to influence them. They want to do what you suggest, even though they don't *have* to.

Ironically, that's much more powerful.

True leaders build their influence by creating relationships with the groups they are called to lead. As the relationships grow, trust emerges. When people trust their leader, good things begin to happen for the team members and for the team, whether we're talking about a team in business or a sports team. In relationships, this investment pays dividends in the areas of team productivity, engagement and satisfaction, while manifesting a higher level of organizational effectiveness.

To put it another way, teams led by a real leader accomplish more and are happier than those driven by a "positional" leader.

Do you want to be an effective leader? If so, build relationships with your team. I'm not discussing friendship or love. I'm talking about listening to your team, treating them with respect, keeping them informed and remaining accessible to them.

This becomes a symbiotic relationship. When your employees see that you're locked in on their concerns and are truly interested in their well-being, you will be able to effect change by influence and not power. This theory holds true wherever and whomever you are called to lead. If you're a businessperson, those relationships may be with a few employees, an entire team or a whole department.

Remember, that example starts with you. Learn to lead yourself and the rest will follow.

Chapter Twenty Five:

Influence, or, "Who's on Your Bus?"

Legendary motivational speaker and author Jim Rohn said, "*You are the average of the five people that you spend the most time with.*"

From my perspective, Mr. Rohn was simply suggesting that those people with whom you associate yourself with influence just about everything that makes up who *you* are. Your *thinking*, your *attitude*, your *behavior*, your *character*, your *reputation*, your *success* and your *happiness* are all directly related to those people to your left and to your right.

Here's how it works. Want to quickly assess the lifestyle of an adolescent? Look at his or her friends. And this not only applies to teenagers, but to those of us who are much older. Humans learn how to think, speak and behave from their environment and those people with whom they share that same environment.

Your environment has everything to do with why you behave the way you do, make the choices you make, and value the things you value. Don't believe me? Try this experiment.

Imagine your life is a bus ride.

Weird? Maybe, but it's my book, so work with me.

Now, if your life is a bus ride, ask yourself, *who is on your bus*? Think about the people currently in your life and do a seat check. Who sits nearest to you? Who is hanging in the back of the bus where bad things happen? What people do you wish would just get off your bus?

Let's start by kicking those people off. Like, now. They can hitchhike home.

Clear your bus of all the negativity, the "can't" folks, the "won't" people, and all of the professional victims (it's not their fault, you know). I'm not suggesting that you remove people that are legitimately reliant upon you like your children and loved ones, but those people in your life that are "drainers," who seem to be there just to suck the life out of you.

There's no room for them on *your* bus.

Kicking the pessimists and negative attitudes and their friends off your bus should leave you with a few empty seats. That means you have room to fill your bus with some new riders of your choosing.

Who gets a ticket? Who do you want to invite along for the ride?

Look for people who share your values, work ethic, positive attitude and energy. Or better yet, offer your empty seats to people who have characteristics to which you aspire. They will begin to influence you in ways that are both obvious and extremely subtle.

If you're the smartest, most positive, highest energy, most honest, most charitable, happiest, and most successful person in your crowd, you need to get a new crowd. You just like to be admired and full of puffery; you're not all that interested in growing as an individual.

The passengers on your bus are the people who will determine where, how fast, and how far that bus is going to go. If they don't challenge you, if they don't motivate you, if they don't enrich your life with welcome additions such as love, friendship, knowledge, wisdom and talent, then why are they there?

I'll let that sit with you for a while. For now, let's pull over because there's something else I want you to look at.

Imagine two parallel rivers, flowing in opposite directions. Luckily, your bus isn't in either one of them, you're just enjoying the view.

Two friends decide to swim a mile in the same direction, one in each river. For the sake of this exercise, we'll assume that these friends possess an identical level of aquatic ability and put forth the same effort in their swimming.

Now, who will reach the finish line first?

Obviously, the friend swimming "with the flow" will reach the goal significantly before the other, who will find the journey to be much harder. In fact, depending upon the flow rate of the rivers, it may be impossible for the friend swimming against the current to actually reach the goal at all.

Recently, I took a ten-day trip where I was surrounded at virtually all times by people with compatible outlooks on life—winning attitudes, love for people and a burning desire to continue to make a positive impact on this world. These were not people without challenges, worries or problems. In fact, there were many amazing stories of overcoming difficulties and aspirations to conquer future challenges. This was a very inspirational experience, and these people were the very kind of people you want on your bus.

Why? In such an environment, it is so much easier to put your life into perspective, to have a renewed sense of purpose and find the resilience to strive toward your goals without worrying about being in control of the outcome. You can simply "go with the flow," but not in the passive, *laissez-faire* sense of the term. The flow is the crowd and *this* crowd helps everyone in it keep moving in the direction they intend to go.

The implication and call to action? Look at your crowd, the "river you're swimming in," the "people on your bus," and give it an honest assessment. Do your surroundings help you to become the person you want to be?

Make sure the passenger list of your bus is comprised of a crowd that's going to get you where you want to go. You'll find it a much more pleasant and speedier journey.

By the way, we haven't even gotten into who's *driving* your bus...

I think we'll save that for the next book.

Chapter Twenty Six:

Channeling my Inner Jeff Foxworthy, or… Coaching 101

I'm no comic, but I love to laugh. I'm also no comedy writer, so sorry if *you* love to laugh. So with that disclaimer now out of the way, I hope you enjoy these amateur one-liners inspired by Jeff Foxworthy's famous "You Might Be a Redneck…" routine:

If you run out of week before you run out of work...you might need a catalyst.

If you're too busy cutting wood to sharpen the saw…you might need a catalyst.

If everyone you know has attended a "How to Deal with Difficult People" seminar…you might need a catalyst.

If the last time you hit the gym was during the Reagan Administration… you might need a catalyst. (If it was the Hoover Administration…hope you enjoyed the greeting from Willard Scott the other morning.)

If you call a 40-hour workweek "half-time"…you might need a catalyst.

If you consider two items from the vending machine a big meal…you might need a catalyst.

If there's never enough time to do it right but always time to do it over… you might need a catalyst.

So are you laughing? If you're not, it's probably because the above jokes weren't funny. Instead, you might just be wondering...*what the heck is a catalyst?*

You should be able to tell I am not a comedy writer because I clearly forget to deliver the "set-up."

In chemistry, a catalyst is a substance that speeds up a chemical reaction without undergoing any permanent chemical change of its own. *It changes other things, but does not change itself.*

That is essentially what I do. I facilitate change that can be sustained without my further involvement. If I was required to sustain the change, that would be building *dependency.* In my work as a catalyst and executive coach, my goal is not to create people who can't function without my help.

Rather, I'm into *independence.* And I make sure my clients are as well.

You may not be sure exactly what an executive coach does, or if you might benefit from working with one, or even the type of coach that is right for you.

The coaching profession is changing so rapidly it's essentially exploding. As a result, there are a wide variety of coaches available from many backgrounds, levels of experience and areas of expertise. It's kind of like the cereal aisle at the supermarket (remember when there was only one kind of Cheerios?).

Now, while the sheer number of coaches may be intimidating to people who are interested in pursuing coaching services, the good news is *there has never been a better time to find a coach that is just right for you.*

Although the exact terminology may vary, coaches work with clients in two fundamental areas—*inner work* and *outer work.*

Inner work focuses on the client's sense of purpose, confidence, values, resilience and beliefs. Effective inner work enables the client to identify and replace self-limiting beliefs and behaviors with newly developed confidence and a powerful attitude.

Outer work is all about performance and results, both at home and in the workplace. This is the domain of goal setting and accountability. The role of the coach here is to inspire and validate the client while providing thoughtful feedback.

Effective coaching consists of many questions, lots of learning and a significant improvement in client outcomes. Coaches often challenge clients to move out of their comfort zones and risk failure in order to take results to the next level.

Neither outer nor inner work is better than the other. The client needs both to succeed over the long haul.

If you asked me how I work with my clients, I first ask questions. Coaching is about questioning, about joint exploration. That questioning and exploration is designed to overcome obstacles and unleash the client's potential to reach goals that are meaningful.

The questions I ask are oriented toward concrete impact and results. They're about helping the client define and then achieve objectives. Rather than looking back in time, my focus is on both *the current situation* and the client's *desired future objective(s).*

So you can gain a better understanding of what I do, here are a dozen of my favorite questions. Try a few on for size:

1. What do you want that you don't presently have?

2. What would the outcome look like?

3. What is your intuition telling you?

4. Where are you putting your energy?

5. Why is this important to you?
6. What will you commit to and when?
7. What is possible or just "a little impossible?"
8. How will you know when you get there?
9. When are you holding back? Giving your best?
10. What might get in the way?
11. What are some other ways to look at the situation?
12. Where do you draw the line? Why there?

And now, one final question:

What do you want from the rest of your life? a) Average? b) Memorable? or c) Incredible?

If your answer was "c," then you might need a catalyst!

Chapter Twenty Seven:

How May I Serve You? The Secret Thing Great Leaders Do (and You Can Too!)

Have you read the book *The Secret?*

Wait one second before you answer that question. I'm not talking about that *Secret.*

The *Secret* I'm talking about isn't about visualization or manifestation, and definitely wasn't on *Oprah*. This *Secret* is about real stuff you do in the real world (not that visualization and manifestation don't have their place in the real world).

Along with Mark Miller, *The Secret* was written by Ken Blanchard, who also authored *One-Minute Manager.* So what's their secret?

Blanchard and Miller's book is all about leadership. The secret that they refer to is the one thing that all great leaders do.

Great leaders *serve* the people who follow them. They serve their employees, their students, their team members, their constituents, and whoever their followers may be.

These leaders may be at the top of their particular heap, but their followers do not serve them. Instead, they **S-E-R-V-E** their followers.

And yes, **S-E-R-V-E** is an acronym.

S-E-R-V-E stands for:

See the Future: Great leaders have a vision for the entire group and convey that vision in a way that stirs passion in their people.

Engage and Develop Others: Great leaders choose their people carefully, put them in the right roles and then invest in them.

Reinvent Continuously: Great leaders have a healthy *disrespect* for the status quo and are always looking for ways to improve and make things better.

Value Results and Relationships: Great leaders don't value one over the other, but recognize that long-term success requires focus on both positive results and personal relationships.

Embody their Values: Great leaders practice what they preach, living out the values that they profess to others in everything they do.

If you have a business, and you want that business to reach the next level, your people must truly serve your customers.

In order to inspire your people to serve, you must first serve *them*. Call it my own management "trickle-down" theory: Lead by example.

The same holds true even if you're not a businessperson or the challenge you're facing isn't business-oriented. For example, if you're a coach who wants his team to win, you should start by serving your players. If you want your volunteer organization to succeed in its mission, you must find a way to inspire the members to serve—and that, again, starts by serving them.

By the way, if you're looking for a read that will serve your quest to *Ascend*, I suggest you check out this less-famous version of *The Secret*. Its full name is *The Secret: What Great Leaders Know—and Do*. It's a quick read, conveys a simple yet powerful message, and, best of all, it focuses on what great leaders really do.

Which will help you become one.

Chapter Twenty Eight:

Is Gratitude Part of Your Attitude?

Author Melody Beattie said, *"Gratitude unlocks the fullness of life. It turns what we have into enough, and more. It turns denial into acceptance, chaos to order, and confusion to clarity. It can turn a meal into a feast, a house into a home, a stranger into a friend."* Gratitude is the manner in which we show appreciation and love for all we have been given. The charity and kindness in others is reflected back onto the world with our gratitude.

There are many events, thoughts, people, relationships, abilities, opportunities and challenges in each of our lives. Part of the experience of ascending is truly feeling gratitude for the gifts you've been given—even those elements of your life that don't exactly appear to be "gifts" at the moment you receive them. It is about recognizing and then celebrating all the good that pokes its way into our lives on a daily basis.

In the winter of 1973, I had heart surgery and missed several months of 5th grade. Yes, I was only ten years old, and no, I didn't have heart problems from smoking and drinking, as my parents drew the line at chocolate milk. I was born with a heart defect and this was a scary time for me and for my family. While it may just be a drop in the bucket in comparison the challenges others may face, I can vividly recall some of the thoughts running through my head during that difficult period.

I was really angry. Angry that God hadn't given me a perfect heart. Angry at kids who were not sick. Angry at the medical personnel that used words I could not understand. Angry that I was missing school. Angry at the old men who were also “heart patients” and looked at me with pity.

It wasn’t supposed to be like this. So I pitied myself too. Looking back, I realize that these were the thoughts and feelings of a scared, selfish child.

Today, I am thankful I had this experience. I am full of gratitude for the thirty-nine years I’ve lived since then. I am even more excited for the years to come. I am grateful for Dr. Cleveland, Dr. Chernoff and the countless other professionals who cared for me, as well as for my parents and brothers who were by my side offering support.

I am also grateful for everything that has happened in my life since then—the wonderful people, the difficult people, the magical moments, and the painful experiences as well.

Okay, maybe not for that time I stepped on a nail and needed to get a tetanus shot. But other than that…nothing but gratitude!

The reality is, wherever you are in life right now, if you take a good, hard, objective look at it, I am 100% positive you will find a long list of things for which to be grateful. In fact, if you take a moment to grab a piece of paper and a pen right now, I’ll bet your list will be so long that you’ll need a *second* piece of paper (or just use the back of the first one—it’s better for the environment!).

Don’t believe me?

Let’s start with the things that keep you alive. How can you not be grateful for the air you breathe, the water you drink and the sun that lights your way and keeps you warm?

Move on to the things you own. Maybe you don’t love your current home, but chances are it does give you a place to sleep at night and take a shower in the morning. And while your car may not be the luxury model of your dreams, chances are it gets you where you want to go.

Whatever else you have, I'm sure you either needed it or wanted it at the time—so you're probably glad to have it.

But stuff is still *just stuff.*

So finish your list (or maybe you should have started your list) with the people you love like your family, your friends, and even the non-human "people" in your life. Perhaps a dog, a cat, or a goldfish. They probably deserve some gratitude as well. As does the stranger who gives up their parking space to you or holds a door open when your hands are full. These small acts of kindness deserve a reciprocal showing of gratitude.

But you are probably considering not just the good, but also those occasions where the not so good presents itself. Internally, you may consider the people that aren't so nice, those items you wish you could purchase, your sad and lonely bank account, or a million other things that annoy you everyday.

My response to that statement?

You can even be grateful for those things. The areas where you perceive your shortfall will inevitably teach you lessons, push you further, keep you grounded and force you to grow.

Focus on what's good in your life. Focus on those things for which you're grateful. And focus on what you can do to bring more of those good things into your life. Blessings are everywhere. Sometimes it just takes looking at your life through a different set of glasses.

And then?

Go out and find some reasons to be even *more* grateful. It's easier than you think.

Chapter Twenty Nine:

Be Happy Now: Don't Be a Sisyphus!

Do you want to be happy?

Most of you reading this will undoubtedly indicate that you do. Unfortunately, this is a *trick* question.

That's because if all you want to be is happy and constantly try to prepare for this happiness, you are unlikely to reach it.

You see, happiness is the ultimate carrot on a stick. Chase it as fast as you might, but it will still remain the same distance in front of you. And happiness is happy to keep that frustrating game going.

"But," you say, "Ed, you tell me to set goals. If I set goals, I can reach them. Well…if happiness is my goal…"

I'm holding up my hand so you can stop there. As I mentioned, I like to run an orderly book.

The fact is I am a big fan of big goals, lofty dreams and ambitious plans. Love them all. But…*happiness is not a goal, dream or a plan.*

Here are a few other things happiness is not. It's not how much money you have. It's not how hot your car is, how big your house is or how many pairs of shoes you own. It's also not how many people you can boss around or who think you're totally awesome.

Happiness is a journey, not a destination—and that journey is represented by *the state of mind you maintain while you're on it.*

How many times have you heard someone say, *"I'll be happy when..."* followed by some random want or need that, once the person acquires it, will leave them just as dissatisfied as before?

Those who subscribe to the myth of *"I'll be happy when..."* are doomed to the fate of Sisyphus. If you don't know who this ancient Greek dude is, check out the picture below:

Sisyphus is the lucky guy pushing the rock up the hill. Now, you might think that, since we're discussing happiness here, Sisyphus will be plenty happy once he finishes pushing that heavy boulder up to the top of that steep hill.

Well, no, not really. Sisyphus is actually a figure of Greek mythology. He may not have even been real. In this legend, he was a King punished for something (I think he may have left the cap off the toothpaste tube one too many times) and therefore, for all eternity, was resigned to push that rock to the top of the hill...*only to see it roll back down again and again.* Rinse and repeat.

And you thought your life was an endless, boring and draining routine.

The point of the story of Sisyphus is to demonstrate that no matter how many times he accomplished the task, he had to do it all over again. The same is true for those people who link their happiness only to achievement—*the happiness just does not last.* Reach the top of the hill and start all over again. Instead, it dissipates like the adrenaline of a workout or the thrills obtained from an exciting movie. In other words, the "happiness boulder" quickly rolls back down the hill, leaving the person to make another long climb back to what he or she considers the pinnacle.

You don't have to be Sisyphus. You don't have Greek Gods controlling your destiny (good thing too—they're good at bringing down the punishment).

You have choices. And you can choose to be happy.

Right now.

So how does that work?

It works when you begin looking beyond the imperfections in your world and focus on the positive parts of your life. No matter the position of your life, there will always be areas of concern, no matter how rich and successful you are. You think Donald Trump's toilet never breaks? Yes, he might have fifty other ones to choose from around the house, but still, even "The Donald" has his fair share of problems.

We all have what's called a "hierarchy of needs." Maybe you just need food and shelter. You get those and soon you start thinking, "Hey, some clothes would be nice." You get clothes, and *then* you begin wondering, "Where do I get a job?" You get a job, and then you want a romantic partner. You get the romantic partner, next it is a nice house to live in and so on and so forth.

It's positively *Sisyphean*. And yes, that is a word.

That's why happiness has to come from within. It sounds like a cliché, but most clichés spring from a place of truth. When we accept the ups and downs of our journey and we focus on the good in our lives and work to make what's not so great better, we allow ourselves a shot at *true, continuous happiness.* We promote the notion that we like where we are now, but we also feel good about where we're headed. The view is nice, but the journey is ongoing.

Now I recognize this is easier said than done, and don't think I don't lose my "happy place" from time to time. But I have a little trick I use to snap my mindset back into place. During a particularly difficult time, *I imagine I have been challenged to remain upbeat.* I hate to lose a contest—so I stave off the negativity and my competitive juices carry me back to a positive state of mind.

A happy person is occasionally sad, just as a sad person is occasionally happy. Things happen to shake us out of our normal moods. In fact, it's part and parcel of being a human being. The important thing is that we make sadness the *temporary* condition—and happiness the *permanent* one.

So let some other guy push the rock up a hill for a while.

Tell 'em you're too busy being happy.

Chapter Thirty:

Leave a Legacy

Sadly, we are at the final chapter of our book-length effort to *Ascend*. At this time, it's highly appropriate that we ponder the notion of "legacy."

You can begin your own personal pondering on this subject simply by imagining what people will say about you when you've ridden into the sunset.

To start, ask yourself these crucial questions:

What lasting impression will you leave with the people who knew you best?

What difference might they say that you made in their lives, in the community, or in the world?

What would you *like* them to say?

What is your purpose?

How do you define success in your life?

I have answered these questions on a personal level numerous times. Having participated in countless conversations on the subject, I can tell you that what I want is to:

1) Live life to my fullest.

2) Love completely and unconditionally.

3) Learn important things (and then do something with the knowledge).

4) Laugh loudly and often, and;

5) *Leave a legacy.*

Those are the big sections in my book, but yours may differ. Whatever the case, the most poignant words on this topic were written by Bessie Stanley. In her poem, "*What Is Success?*" she said:

"To laugh often and love much; to win the respect of intelligent persons and the affection of children; to earn the approbation of honest citizens and endure the betrayal of false friends; to appreciate beauty; to find the best in others; to give of one's self; to leave the world a bit better, whether by a healthy child, a garden patch or a redeemed social condition; to have played and laughed with enthusiasm and sung with exultation; to know even one life has breathed easier because you have lived...this is to have succeeded."

The success gurus always say, "You should work *on* your business, not just *in* your business?" While I believe this to be great advice, I am confident you should consider taking that maxim a step further and work *on* your life, not just *in* your life.

When it comes to your legacy, in addition to your day-to-day planning for the next few weeks, also spend some time reflecting on the legacy you've built *thus far.*

Now carefully compare that to the legacy you'd like to *eventually* leave the world.

Where are the gaps? What can you do about them?

What strengths can you utilize to bridge the gap?

What's the best first step?

When will you take that step?

This is the standard goal-setting process, applied to possibly the most precious goal of all—achieving a lasting legacy. If you're like me, you want your life to end up being viewed as a gift that improved the world, even if in only a very small way.

If you take the time to do this exercise, I promise you that you'll be well on your way to achieving *true* success in your life and leaving your mark on the world.

That's the ultimate way to *Ascend* to perfection in your life, your work and in your most precious relationships.

Now…up, up and away!

Afterword:

Which Do You Choose?

"The king is the man who can."
- Keith Richards

"The queen is the woman who can."
- Ed DeCosta (who wants to make sure all bases are covered)

I hope you've enjoyed our quest of ascent in the pages of this book. I do want to mention that all of the preceding chapters are based on blogs I've written over the past few years, so, if you're sad this book is coming to a close, fear not—because there are plenty *more* new entries for your perusal on my website at www.eddecosta.com.

I have a few final thoughts I'd like to share before this book comes to a close. To begin with, if there's a word that I believe sums up the theme of this book, that word is *"Potential."* Potential is within all of us. It is just a matter of tapping into it and firing it up.

I've used the word many times in this book and, undoubtedly, you've heard it many times outside of this book, possibly even directed at you. Most often, it seems we hear this word used in reference to a young person or athlete. After all, your younger years are when you appear to have the greatest opportunity to reach your potential. You rarely see a 90-year-old described as having a lot of potential (although I personally never count anybody out!).

However, the flip side here is that many times the term "potential" is used to manifest a negative assessment. A judgment like "unfulfilled potential" can be a devastating label, and usually very hurtful to the person in question. Since *nobody* really knows your potential, *you* probably don't even fully grasp what your own potential is or may be.

Sure, you have some God-given abilities and skills, and maybe even some you developed after thousands of hours of life experience, study and hard work. But have you reached your *potential*? Have you achieved what you're really capable of?

The ancient Greeks praised many virtues, but none more than "*arête.*" Arête refers to excellence, fulfillment of purpose, living up to one's potential and being the best that an individual can be.

How much *arête* do you have in your tank?

Let's try and find out.

We began this book with what I call my "DVD exercise," where I asked you to look at an imaginary DVD containing video highlights of your life years from now. Your job was to determine what you wanted to see in those highlights.

Well, I'd like to now close with a similar exercise—one that centers more on who you are and what you stand for.

Fire up your imagination one last time for me. Picture yourself looking into a classroom where *30 alternative versions* of you are sitting at desks. All of these versions are from the future—let's say five years from now—and each "Future You" is a realistic possibility.

In other words, none of them have superpowers, nor are they a member of the Royal Family of England, and none of them are on a reality television show.

Now, some of those 30 Future Yous are not so appealing. They represent who you might become should you make five years of poor choices or even show a complete lack of discipline or focus. Let's call these the "Unfulfilled Potentials."

However, there are many other Future Yous in the room that appear to be amazing. They represent the *best possible* physical, emotional, social, spiritual, financial, and intellectual *versions* of you. These Future Yous also demonstrate the amazing positive impact you've had on the lives of others. Let's call these the "Full Potentials."

(By the way, you've probably noticed that there's still one sitting there who doesn't fit into either category. That's because that Future You didn't change *at all* in five years. As a consequence, there's been a demotion—that Future You has been downgraded to just plain old *You*.)

Now here comes your exercise: *Can you visualize the exact version of the ideal you that you'd like to become?*

Concentrate on that version. Write down what you "see" in that particular Future You.

Which you did you choose? Why?

Now, describe what this Future You will be like, feel like, and think like? What will the life of this Future You resemble?

Take your time and really think this through.

And most importantly, how did this wonderful, incredible Future You come to fruition?

What did you have to do to bring this version of yourself to life?

If you can fully imagine this Future You and what it took to create him or her, then you can start to create a plan to begin the shift to make this version of yourself a reality. And maybe this Future You can arrive in your skin a little sooner than five years from now.

After all, if this Future You is so great, why wait if you don't have to? There's no reason to delay.

The *best possible version of you* is ready to be created.

And I sincerely hope I get to meet that awesome person one day.

About the Author

Ed DeCosta is co-author of *Mastering the Art of Success* with Jack Canfield, and now author of *ASCEND: A Coach's Roadmap for Taking Your Performance to New Heights.* He is President of Catalyst Associates LLC, an executive coaching and management consulting firm. Catalyst Associates helps clients set and achieve ambitious goals, enabling them to meet their personal and business objectives. Clients range from entrepreneurial ventures to Fortune 500 corporations.

In his corporate years, Ed managed worldwide sales and marketing teams and opened offices on three continents. He is presently working as a partner with best-selling author and leadership guru John C. Maxwell, serving as one of the faculty members on the leadership development program called the John Maxwell Team.

He is an ICF certified executive coach, has a B.S. in Mechanical Engineering from West Virginia University, as well as Masters Degree in International Management and MBA from the University of Texas. Ed is also an adjunct faculty member in WVU's College of Business and Economics, teaching Professional Selling and Entrepreneurship courses.

A native of Boston and a diehard fan of the Boston Red Sox, Ed now makes his home in the rolling hills near Morgantown, West Viginia with his wife Linda and their 3 children.

For more, visit www.eddecosta.com

Made in the USA
Middletown, DE
29 October 2016